Freedom Is -

(period.)

by Dr. Robert C. Worstell

(this book also published as part of
"Go Thunk Yourself, Revisited".)

Cover art based on photography by Johnathan Gill -
"Sitting on the Fence"
(http://www.flickr.com/photos/jonathangill/3581405155/)

Beta release 0.1

This book is partially based on essays and articles originally
posted on "A Midwest Journal" (http://robertworstell.com) and
are used with the author's permission.

Table of Contents

Disclaimer

No part of this publication may be reproduced, stored in a retrieval system, or transmitted in any form or by any means, electronic, mechanical, photocopying, recording, scanning, or otherwise, except as permitted under Section 107 or 108 of the 1976 United States Copyright Act, without the prior written permission of the Author.

Limit of Liability/Disclaimer of Warranty: While the publisher and the author have used their best efforts in preparing this book, they make no representations or warranties with respect to the accuracy or completeness of the contents of this book and specifically disclaim any implied warranties of merchantability or fitness for a particular purpose. No warranty may be created or extended by sales representatives or written sales materials. The advice and strategies contained herein may not be suitable for your situation. You should consult with a professional where appropriate. Neither the publisher nor the author shall be liable for any loss of profit or any other commercial damages, including but not limited to special, incidental, consequential, or other damages.

(Don't you just love how lawyers have it set up? Your mileage may vary. Caution, contents may be hot...)

Part I - Masterworks on Personal Freedom

-o0o-

Prelude

Our quest for personal Freedom is really illustrated well in this tale of the misadventures of a young Ivy League professor.

The story begins with an academic who was researching in his university's antiquities archive in the early 1900's and came across a misfiled piece of parchment. While it was in an ancient language, it was readable to this well-studied young man. It told of a repository of incredible knowledge which was found at the top of a remote mountain. In this place would be found all secrets revealed, all mysteries explained. The professor cross-referenced this data and found little except intriguing clues that the parchment was indeed authentic, and apparently hundreds of years old, and that the area it refers to is also known by other texts as a forbidden area with many dangers. No accurate maps of the area existed at that time. And legends he consulted backed this up with tales of a mysterious mountain where people would lose their mind in searching for knowledge and power. As well, that these secrets were stored in this one location for the good of humankind, to keep them safe and secure.

As the professor continued his research, this became a consuming passion with him. It started to invade his dreams at night - where he often found himself alone on a barren mountainside, ever climbing, despite torn clothes and scraped fingers, with a piercing, freezing cold wind that tried to pluck him off his tenuous perch down into the depths below.

Even his friends note his haggard look. His students start spreading stories about lectures where this young professor simply stopped in mid-sentence, looking off into the distance - transfixed by what he was thinking about.

The professor finally realized that something must be done. He arranged finances for this journey, calling in all his favors and confiding with key university donors about what he expected to find on this mountain top - the secrets to all knowledge, all powers of the universe explained.

Finally, he had just enough to cover a single person on this excursion, one his Dean called "foolhardy" even as he scrawled his approval for that professor's emergency sabbatical request.

Leaving notes for his friends and family, telling his landlady to not disturb his room while he was away, the professor hurriedly departed. His itinerary required him to take steamship, railways, and finally both mule- and llama-trains to the remote area where legend said the mysterious mountain sat. As he traveled, he asked the locals about the legend - did they believe it, where did they think it was. Most hadn't heard of it. Those that did just smiled and shook their head, telling him nothing more.

But as he traveled deeper inland, he found more and more people smiling and saying nothing. He knew he was getting closer and concluded these locals evidently were just keeping all these secrets to themselves. A few told him what he was looking for was incredibly dangerous - that the climb had often turned back those individuals who had tried. The mountain was treacherous, with screaming winds that tore climbers loose from their grip, and always shrouded in dark and forbidding clouds. They told of people who had never returned from the climb, leaving their belongings at the nearest inn, unclaimed. And others who returned forever haunted by what they had seen, strange looks etched into their faces...

Finally, the professor reached the remote valley which his research said lay just below the base of this mountain. Descending on foot down a zig-zag path cut into the hillside, he noticed that the valley was well organized into farms like a patchwork quilt as far as he could see. While the mountains surrounding the valley were cloaked in clouds, the valley itself was well-lit with plenty of sunshine for the growing crops.

Freedom Is (period.) - 5

There was one building for visitors, an inn of sorts, with rooms to let. In the main room were climbing gear hung on the walls - some ancient, some modern. One caught the professor's eye – it bore the inscription of a famous explorer who had disappeared in this area just a few years earlier. Yet it looked like it hadn't been used, just left for the innkeeper to care for against the owner's eventual return.

As his evening meal was brought, he asked his server about the legend. The old man's brow furrowed with worry and he silently looked deep into the professor's eyes - then the worry was replaced with laughter lines as his face lit up into a broad smile. But still, the old man wouldn't say anything about the legend. Instead, he merely asked, "You starting at first light?"

The professor nodded. The old server just chuckled and turned, hobbling back to the cook-room.

That night's sleep was restless, the old dreams returned. As he climbed the mountain in his dream, he made a careless error and grabbed a loose rock formation which crumbled in his hand. Just then the wind ripped fiercely across his back and buffeted him loose. He stumbled and then began falling -- falling down into the foggy depths, flailing arms and legs finding no purchase.

The young professor awoke, sweating, as he "landed" in his soft bed at the inn. The first pale glimmers of light were starting to show and he heard the tinkling of bells as the herders arranged their goats for milking and feeding.

Dressing quickly, he almost inhaled his breakfast and went to thank his host, who was standing near the doorway. As his innkeeper opened the door, he stopped the professor. One hand on his visitor's shoulder, the old man raised his arm and pointed to the nearest end of the valley - where the professor could see a clear path that wound through and finally disappeared as it rose up into the low morning fog.

An easy walk, this fit academic wasn't even breathing hard as he reached the far valley end, and he saw this path become thinner and less defined as it took him up beyond the valley's edge and into the waiting clouds above. Looking up, he could only make out glimpses of the mountain side. He found himself at the edge of the treeline now, and only very shrubby, small plants held onto life in and amongst the rocks and boulders.

Suddenly, a touch on his elbow caused him to whirl. There stood a bent old man with a staff, his goats behind him. The man said nothing, but looked solemn. But then a slight, even wistful smile crossed his craggy face. He began to speak with a broken dialect, which the professor understood as composed from several ancient languages he'd only studied in his archives.

This goat-herder told him that the path ended here. He'd have to make his own way from this point. He pointed up the mountainside, a direction to take up to the top. The professor tried to peer through the clouds covering that direction, but when he turned back to ask for more directions, the old man was gone. The young professor was alone.

The next long hours were just as his dreams had forewarned. Sharp outcroppings tugged and ripped his clothes, while scraping his hands. The wind was gusting and severe, the clouds thick and cold - he often would lose sight of his own feet as he climbed on and on,up and up. But his feared nightmares didn't happen. He climbed precisely and relentlessly, careful to place each foot solidly, and ensuring each handhold was firm and secure.

Finally, he reached a point where there was no more "up". Casting about in all directions, he could not find another, higher grip. Moving carefully around the mist-shrouded rock, he could find no other hand or foot-hold which would lead to any higher level. Had he reached the top? Where was this monastery he thought to be here, or was some ancient book or roll of parchment buried somewhere near?

The wind increased precipitously. He quickly shrank back to secure his hold and footing, closing his eyes to concentrate on holding his place against the severe buffeting. It was then the light got brighter and the wind ceased.

He opened his squinted eyes slowly - to find himself holding on to a rock in the middle of a field, with flat pasture all around. It was a sunny day and goats were grazing contentedly about. Instead of mountain, there was only the broad field covered with native grasses and brush. A few feet away, he saw a goat-herder - who turned toward him at the same time.

Rising from the rock, the professor wiped his scraped hands on his shredded tunic and walked over to the goat-herder.

Surprisingly, it was the same face the professor had seen at the top edge of the valley. "Where am I, where's the mountain?" he shouted.

The goat-herder smiled and replied quietly to that young academic, "You are here, you made it."

Perplexed, the professor asked, "But I was climbing a mountain - where is it?"

The goat-herder smiled even more broadly and said simply, "There never was a mountain. You were here all the time.

"Congratulations - you've now arrived."

Forward

The story in the preceding pages illustrates the exact point which lead me finally to write this last book. As the professor discovered, Freedom Is - (period.).

Through all the books I've studied and lectures listened to - as well as my own research and tests down this line — it has become very clear to me that *we each already have all the, Freedom, Happiness, and Peace we could ever want,* It's just sitting there waiting for us to recognize its presence in our nature. Just waiting for us to let our own light shine.

That's the secret people have been looking for all this time, the one which the self-help guru's will sell you unlimited books, CD's, video's, and personal consultation to help you find. But I think, like Dorothy with her slippers, you eventually find that you've had the solution all along. And also like Dorothy, you have to make the journey before you'll believe it's that simple.

This is the route to enlightenment which people have chased for so long, one which has lead some people around in circles, others to an early grave. Throughout the ages, enlightenment has been sought, and sometimes found. But these efforts often were hidden in musty archives. It's only been in this Internet Age that anyone can have access to vast amounts of data, both ancient and modern, literally at one's fingertips.

It has become not only easier, but absolutely vital that each person take what can be grasped and experienced from this "virtual buffet", and let the rest go. (Just as a thirsty person can't use the full output of a fire hose.) With all these resources so immediately available, any idea of having "the truth" dictated by any single person to anyone else shows up as pretense. And as you now have to choose for yourself, the truth within will to start shining out on its own.

The trick is this one, simple datum:

The limits you have, the only things holding you back, are those you have accepted.

And these limits are all additive, not natural.

All the Freedom, Happiness, and Peace you want is already found within you, so to speak. It isn't found by attending certain political rallies, or as a martyr for some cause. There is no government which can guarantee you any amount of freedom. No amount of money can buy it. No specific inherited DNA allows you to have more or less Freedom than the next fellow. And, likewise, no external person or thing can, of itself, actually limit your Freedom, even in the slightest.

The amount of Freedom, Happiness, and Peace you can have is dependent on yourself. You set your own limits to what you experience, every second of every day in your lifetime.

Check out any number of biographies and you will find these certain facts. The person's beliefs limit him more than any upbringing, family wealth - or lack of it. No particular race of people has had more enduring freedom than any other.

What is true of freedom is also true of financial abundance, prosperity, good health, loving relationships. Name a humankind condition of lack or want and you will find that the person themselves actually set their own limits to what they could personally be, do, or have.

However, the solutions to these conditions have been repetitively re-discovered and republished throughout history. Study all the self-help authors you can come across. Download and distill all their books into simple basics and you will find (at least in the true bestsellers) a common theme and common approaches to these problems.

And it's not just self-help. Take those distilled approaches and see if the myths and legends of history and pre-history don't abound with the same principles. Where there was any success, heroes and heroines were able to discard the accepted "conventional wisdom" and replaced it with their own unlimited ideas of success - which they then followed to make their mark in history.

Backtrack all the (1) financial wizards and the multi-billionaires who travel or have traveled this earth. You'll find in each of them these same principles of unlimited wealth. Look up the people known as "healers" and you'll see they also subscribe to these principles, and their successes as healers are generally only with the treated individuals who also subscribe and put their faith in these ideas of unlimited health. Where you can, seek out people who get along with everyone they meet. Interview them and you'll find that they all agree that there isn't anyone they can't get along with - unlimited successful relationships.

- - - -

What are these principles - and how long does it take a person to find them?

Well, for most people, it can take an entire lifetime just to distill these. Others seem to be "lucky" and stumble onto them right off the bat.

For me, after a half-century of living on this planet, I've spent the bulk of it in searching and studying for just these principles. The last decade has been devoted to simplifying them down to a single core set, which anyone could apply. In this last year, I finally uncovered the missing perspective which should enable profound progress for anyone.

And so I sat down to write about it, because it's just too wonderful to keep to myself.

What's being laid before you isn't necessarily an easy task, while it is simple. It might involves a considerable amount of work on your part. Some may find that their results come easy, others may find that what they are trying to achieve seems nearly impossible. And no two people find they have to invest the same amount of time, or that they can even get similar results by applying the identical data. As the cliché goes "Results May Vary."

Several old sayings are applicable:

1. The ancient Japanese would say: "There are many paths up the mountain."

2. The ancient Polynesians tell: "No one school has all the teachers."

These, together, tell of a story which is different for every single person on this planet. Just as we are all unique from each other (and even as identical twins have their own separate identities) so do we each have a unique path that we must find for ourselves to make this path up our own mountain to attain whatever Freedom, Happiness, and Peace we truly seek. Consider this book simply an effort to share various climbing tools.

So why, then, would I try to write a book outlining a common series of principles, only to tell you that it's different for everyone of us?

While it varies in the details, your path still aligns to certain natural laws which cannot be changed by any individual within this Universe we live in. Those people who have learned or stumbled across these natural laws and worked out how to apply them for their own existence on this planet - these have found out how to create any amount of anything they want to be, do, or have in their lives.

What I won't tell you here is that if you only apply a single law, like the Law of Attraction, or the Golden Rule, that either or both of these – or any other singular "law" - will make you rich, famous, successful, etc.

What you find as you climb your own mountain will be exactly what you want and need to find. And only you can do the climbing, and you are the one who must choose which branch, fork, or side trail to take as you climb. Not all will be fruitful. Some will be dead-ends, and you will have to backtrack. You're going to have to keep your eyes open for opportunities and be willing to learn and profit from the lessons coming your way. If you're like me, your "dead-ends" will teach you more than you can imagine.

But the only things which are keeping you from what you really want to be, do, or have - all that Freedom, Happiness, and Joy you seek - is only within yourself. Ideas and thought-processes and world-views which you've accepted over the years have been piled higher and deeper to get the exact result of where you sit right now.

What you see around you is what you've created. And if you want something better, you're going to have to re-create that world around you.

- - - -

As we go along through this book, I'll try to keep it interesting, try to keep it short and useful.

In this book, I'm giving you the climbing tools you can use if you want to improve your life with, all drawn from all these famous authors and their stories which we'll cover as we go.

All you really see here is the best path I've been able to determine for myself as I make my way up my own mountain. But my path, I've found, depends on enabling you to find yours.

While I'm proud of the work represented here, and I believe that this book represents a rather unique approach, I don't write it out of any idea that I'm the first to walk this way, or that I'm even particularly very far along the path myself. I don't even write it with the idea that this book is any better than the books I mention and review here.

And while I consider that an important part of my life-path is sharing what I've found, the only one who can say this is truly useful, is you. Take none of this as gospel, just consider it as you can, and decide for yourself what you want to believe after you've tested it.

Each of us needs help from time to time as we make our way along. I've had plenty, and it's time to give back. Or, you can take it another way - "A person has to give before they can get." Meaning that where I or anyone else wants to improve their life, there has to be a lot of giving in order to make these things come about.

So this book is my gift to you. Pay it forward in advance yourself. See if it doesn't help you get to where you want to wind up - or maybe someplace even better...

Introduction

In this book, we are overing six authors: whose data you should know, understand, and apply in your life.

Many you have heard of, if you haven't already studied them at length:

Napoleon Hill - "Think and Grow Rich" as well as "Law of Success"

Charles F. Haanel - "Master Key System"

Wallace Wattles - "Science of Getting Rich"

Earl Nightingale - "The Strangest Secret" and his "Lead the Field" series

Serge Kahili King - "Urban Shaman" and "Mastering Your Hidden Self"

Lester Levenson - discoverer of the Levenson releasing technique

Individually, any one of these might be used to gain your own enlightenment, to gain whatever you want to be, do, or have in your lifetime and profoundly improve your life. This is highlighted by their continuing success and/or best-seller status. Each has devoted followings who are constantly reviewing their books, recordings, and any videos that exist by or about them and their teachings.

Put all together, though, they make an incredibly formidable approach to solving life's mysteries and eliminating all lacks from anyone's life. A study of these teachers takes on an even more profound character.

In this short book, I've included descriptions or actual excerpts from their books so that you can study and learn and improve your life with what I consider Life's core principles. These few principles can be used toward whatever goals you might have. Or they may help in the search for ultimate truth itself. What you'll see here are digests of their material so that you can take the key points for immediate application to start right now and begin improving your life.

Take what I say here as "just for checking." My continuing advice is to get these authors' books and read them at the same time you do this one. So you can check for yourself whether you've discovered a truth.

To my understanding, these six authors' works comprise a "universal solvent" for any of the humankind situations we all find ourselves in. A Universal Solvent has the problem of dissolving any container you try to put it in. The only practical container would have to be created out of the substance itself.

For you, I'm offering this route of study so that you can quickly determine your own path in order to release the native Freedom, Happiness, and Joy that already lies within you.

One of the key results I hope you will gain from this work is the understanding that nothing can be held secret from you, that you can readily find all solutions you need, that any situation you find yourself in can be readily resolved. In short, no external influence can stop you or slow you down from here on out.

Certainly, I won't say that this will be easy, or that whatever you want will show up tomorrow. You have to walk your own path.

But I can and do say that these six authors - studied carefully - will bring a new level of enlightenment to anyone who studies them. And that all who do will be able to achieve a very high level of personal Freedom within this certain lifetime, but only if they really want a clear connection to the highest truths available to man. And as you work out your paths with these high truths, life can't help but improve beyond measure.

It depends on you and what you want to do. How hard you want to work at it. How much you want to help others succeed around you.

But, before you dig in, there are two important things to keep in mind:

1. If you can't seem to connect to any particular section or author, move on. Don't get stuck. This is not a certain or prescribed study sequence, it's an invitation to explore.

2. However much you might try, you can't get this wrong. Any "wrong turn" will always eventually lead you where you need to go, all the more fulfilled. So relax and welcome whatever (and I really do mean absolutely whatever) happens as you apply what you find.

Both of these ideas spring from something I discovered along the way: Truth is experiential. You can't get it from books or gurus, preachers or schools. You alone can determine it for yourself. Truth can have no copyright or trademark or patent. When you do understand a fundamental truth, you can thereafter see it everywhere and hear it from many different sources. These truths are all around you. But until you see them for yourself, you won't notice.

This book is not about my truth, or the truths any or all of these authors explored. It is about the truth that's always been with you, that's always been part of you. It's not about learning new things, really. It's about learning to let the truth that is already within you to start shining forth.

I sincerely hope you find this effort useful.

Robert C. Worstell

Mar 17, 2010

Napoleon Hill - Fuel A Burning Desire

Napoleon Hill met an interesting person on one of his very first assignments as a reporter for a small country newspaper. And what was supposed to be an hour-long interview stretched out three days. At the end of this, he accepted a non-paid commission which lasted 20 years and affected him the rest of his life – giving him continuing successes.

Andrew Carnegie was his first interview subject. Carnegie had an odd request. He saw something in Hill that could make it possible. Carnegie's commission: to interview 500 famous and successful person and, from these collected and varied life experiences, distill a single practical success formula anyone could apply to improve their own quality of life.

For Hill, this was an incredible opportunity. Hill had been born in a one-room log cabin in southwest Virginia. And tells in his books about the various tough times his family had on a dirt-poor farm. He had made it through school and got onto a backwoods newspaper as a cub reporter, looking for a big break – and this could be it.

However, Carnegie only offered to reimburse him for out-of-pocket expenses – and he was to interview over 500 of the most famous people of that time to distill their own success principles. But the rest is history.

Almost exactly 20 years after that Carnegie interview, Hill reached the point of distilling these interview into a single philosophy in 1928. While he published this in a home-study course titled "The Law of Success", his real personal success was when he set about to solve the main problem the "Great Depression" had – and why he felt it was continuing. And from this 16-volume set, he distilled a single book that could be easily understood by the man on the street with just an average education. Titled "Think and Grow Rich", this went on to become perhaps the best selling self-help book in America.

In this book, Hill wrote about how to essentially recession-proof your life. He gave a simple way to always wind up a financial and material success if you just know and follow these few principles.

Hill had 13 points to his masterpiece which went far beyond just becoming rich or prosperous

In short:

1. Develop a burning desire for your life.

2. Develop your faith in yourself.

3. Use auto-suggestion to reprogram your mind.

4. Obtain the specialized knowledge you need.

5. Strengthen your creative imagination.

6. Utilize organized planning toward your goal.

7. Reach decisions promptly - and stick to them..

8. Develop and practice persistence.

9. Develop a Master Mind group of associates.

10. Recognize Love as a driving force.

11. Utilize your subconscious mind

12. Use your brain as an antenna for broadcasting and receiving inspiration.

13. Welcome Sixth Sense input.

Think and Grow Rich was boiled down from his earlier master-work, "Law of Success". Carnegie knew there was a common theme present, as he'd seen it with his own eyes when he climbed from the steel-working floor up to owner. And also knew that the government-run schools weren't training it - as he hired people with little formal education, who then became leaders of men and millionaires in their own right.

Law of Success was the core book series behind Think and Grow Rich. Hill produced this last to help the world throw off the remaining vestiges of the Great Depression. What he did was to create a handbook which went far beyond merely amassing money, but became a modern classic which probably one out of every three people has read or knows someone who has read this book and uses its data.

We can boil that bestseller down to even simpler core principles which repeat through his book - so we can then use those to re-build our own life into what we've always wanted.

The key point is concentrating on the core desire or life-purpose you want to achieve.

This is the idea behind Hill's BURNING DESIRE.

A deep, driving desire - developed by constantly reminding yourself.

And here we have Hill's use of Coue's auto-suggestion. While I'll cover more effective approaches later, this use of affirmations is commonly employed today - as it's a very useful tool.

Hill suggested 6 steps to formulating this burning desire. While his approach in this book was to remedy the widespread fear of lack, it will do for any goal:

1. Fix in your mind the exact amount of money you desire.

2. Determine what you intend to give in return.

3. Establish a definite date when you intend to possess that sum.

4. Create a definite plan and begin at once.

5. Write out a clear, concise statement of the amount, it's date certain to have it, what you intend to give in return, and describe your plan clearly.

6. Read your written statement aloud, twice daily (evening before bed and very first thing in the morning - and feel yourself already in possession of the money.

It's really that simple - and millions have put this sequence or some variation to work in their own lives with incredible success.

There are reasons this works.

A. Any lack of accomplishing anything is simply due to dispersal instead of concentration. Once you concentrate everything you have, all your abilities, into a single channel of attention, then you will eliminate or handle every single obstacle that comes in between you and your goal. The key word is concentration.

B. You have to give before you can get. Nothing appears out of the blue, exactly. You'll find people had already been giving far more than they had to. They spent extra time and attention on the job at hand to make sure that it was of far more value than was requested. So their employer got more than was paid for. Anything they sold was far better quality and a lower price than it was obviously worth - a true bargain.

C. Plan your work, work your plan. If the plan doesn't work, then revise and start it again - immediately. That's the key. Get started right now on what you should be doing. Don't think it over any further. Strike while the iron is hot. And stick to that plan until you run into something unworkable, or something you hadn't foreseen - then rework the plan and go hammer-and-tongs at it again. Immediately.

D. Remind yourself daily of exactly where you are going, what you are giving, what you are doing, and realize it's already there and already yours - that all your steps are just making it arrive faster. You have to develop a calm knowing that all you really want is already there. That's the reason for the note and reading it daily.

And we can then add additional steps, which are less approved by our common society, but are incredibly more effective than anything we've ever tried to learn in schools:

E. Connect with the Infinite daily. Practice your intuition skills and they will improve. Don't rely on your thinking to carry you through, but be willing to look beyond your analytical thoughts right through to your creative core - and tap into this endless source for your own brilliant flashes of solution.

F. Realize that the love you feel and share for those around you is key to your connection to the Infinite - it serves as motivation and reward. As you develop this appreciation, it will grow. And all those you work with will be able to share in this - their own intuitive skills will bring you new data and approaches which you can all share toward your common goals. Creative imagination runs on love, which is the most vital and primal force in this universe - and which is responsible for creating all you see around you.

G. Work with what you know and never second-guess it. While we'll deal with this later, the key point now is to follow Hill's suggestion and just make your decisions quickly and stick to it. Your first idea is more often than not your best idea. Get it done. Once you teach yourself this discipline, it simplifies your life - things speed up as you get more efficient.

H. Join, build, and form an association of like-minded individuals. Both immediately around you in terms of associates at your work-place, and also meetings you can attend at remote locations annually or more frequently. This would also include people you might meet online and can only converse with through that medium. Such an association will reinforce your common goals and gain far more together than the individual parts of it could. This is Hill's Master Mind.

- - - -

Now, of course, I could sit and write chapters on each point above - but that's what Hill did, after all. What we bring here is analysis and boiling down the key points - which we'll start tying together as we continue through all these famous bestseller authors.

Where you study and restudy Hill's master-work ("Think and Grow Rich" or "Law of Success"), you'll come to a greater understanding and use of his data. If you only studied Hill alone, anything you wanted would be yours.

I have other authors to present to you, however. When you get these others' secrets made into your own, absorbed into your new operating basis - then you will see a much larger pattern that works even faster than any single author included in this volume.

So let me introduce and discuss our next author who mapped out how the entire universe operates in a single book with 24 lessons...

Charles F. Haanel - Understand The Universal System

A completely self-made success, Charles Hannel started and built companies in the US and Mexico, all before the cusp of 1900 had turned. And his success in these would have been unremarkable but for the fact he sat down to figure out and write up a breakthrough correspondence course so that anyone with tuition could also learn to succeed in their own lives.

Born in Michigan, his family moved to St. Louis, Missouri during his childhood. One of his first jobs was with a factory in that city where he worked in various positions there for 15 years, before setting out his on his own career. Rising to leadership in a coffee and sugar plantation in Tehuantepec Mexico, he built this company into one of the largest conglomerates of its day. As well, he became President of the Sacramento Valley Improvement Company, which owned the largest Tokay vineyards in the world. He was also member of several clubs and received several honorary degrees.

He wrote the Master Key System at the age of 43 and first promoted it through New Thought magazines in 1909 as a mail-order course. The tuition was $1,000. As popular as it was, he converted it to a printed book in 1912 and went on to sell 200,000 copies worldwide by 1933.

Napoleon Hill thanked Haanel in a letter for the material he had written in his Master Key System – saying that his success with the Napoleon Hill Foundation was due to following Haanel's principles.

Charles Haanel's Master Key System is unique and advanced beyond it's simple 24 lessons. This could probably be titled, "Your Guide to How the Universe Actually Works." And my restudy of it for this short book brings me to new understandings of it as a basic book that everyone should have in their library for continual and regular reference.

Owing to it's sheer volume of data, this section may seem longer than others. But when you are dealing with the universe, that's still a lot of information to boil down. Factually, I only bring you the tips of the icebergs of knowledge which sit in each chapter. It is up to you to learn and study Haanel's basics for yourself, paragraph by paragraph.

1. Anything is possible to achieve or acquire, if you only develop the consciousness to understand them.

You only need live in the spirit of what you want or need or would just like to appear. To one who knows, the universe is not static, but fluid - and able to flow anything in your direction.

You already have this power - you only have to learn how to let it shine, which means becoming one with it.

As you work with this material, you will find that your inspiration will deepen, your plans will crystallize, and you will gain a deeper understanding that this world is a living thing - composed of the living entities which exist on it. It's a creation of life and beauty.

Once you work from this certain knowledge, you will be inspired deeply and gain greater confidence and ability every day - realizing not only your hopes and dreams as they come true, but that "life has a deeper, fuller, clearer meaning than before."

2. Any problems or difficulties or situations are simply the ignorance of the laws of nature. So a clear mind and direct intuition are invaluable.

As you work to clear your mind, your rewards are greater and you reach for even higher goals. Your abilities heighten as you study and gain understanding of the best that has been thought - and so your personal pleasure heightens to the supreme levels.

With this new understanding of the mind's process, there are possibilities which are far beyond what material science has brought so far:

"Thought is energy. Active thought is active energy; concentrated thought is a concentrated energy." ✱!

When you concentrate your mind on a definite purpose, anything is achievable, anything can be acquired. There is no longer any reason for poverty or lack.

Your abilities to use the mind-power you already possess depends upon your ability to recognize the infinite energy which is in and around you, which is ready to manifest anything you need at a moment's notice. And it will manifest to you in the exact proportion you understand it, and your willingness to apply it.

3. The individual can act on the Universal: thinking in the mind as the cause, and your life experiences as effect.

So it's a waste of time to complain about how things are or how they have been, because its up to you to change them into what you really want. You have to concentrate on mastering your mind and all your vast mental resources.

Through persistence, you'll find that only success is possible when you direct your mind toward accomplishing any object or goal. As you persist, and apply what you know, all your mental abilities align to bring that accomplishment into fact.

The trick and method is to make your new mental actions into new habits, which then train the subconscious, and so free the mind up to take on other activities.

4. There is a single indication of what you are - it's your mind and how you use it.

For all history, attention has only been given to the effects of this mental energy and not on understanding, controlling, and harnessing the energy itself. The world has been concentrating on the effect, not the cause.

And so the concentration on dichotomies such as God and the Devil, Good and Bad, etc.

Living is full of constructive and harmonious action. There is no practical reason for sorrow, misery, unhappiness, disease, and poverty. These are being regularly eliminated, if slowly.

To do this, a person has to rise among considering limits of any kind. Fate, Fortune, and Destiny are as easily controlled as a ship by its captain, or an airplane by its pilot.

5. This is a creative age we live in - and those who are using their mind to consider new thoughts are receiving the richest rewards.

Matter is passive and inert, while Mind is energy and active. Mind shapes and controls matter. All the forms in matter are just an expression of earlier mental action.

The mind works through natural laws and activate natural motions, natural energies. What happens around you is the result of your original thoughts and thinking - your use of your own mind to create the world around you.

> *"You can originate thought, and, since thoughts are creative, you can create for yourself the things you desire."*

6. Any degree of Health, Success, Prosperity, or anything else you want is already yours.

This world is under continual evolution, constant change toward improvement. Your own development is also gradual and ever increasing in your own expanding abilities.

The warning here comes from the certain knowledge that where we hurt others, where we impede their success, we affect our own to that same degree. So there is the simple action of always working for the greater good, the highest ideals - not only for ourselves, but for everyone around us.

And working for the highest possible achievements, the best and most harmonious relationships - this will bring about the results you seek. Only lies and fixed ideas will hold you back.

To get the best for ourselves, we must be personally in harmony with ourselves. You have to be in touch with the Universe.

Thoughts are just products of your mind, which is naturally creative. Just because you are creative, this doesn't mean that the Universe will immediately respond. But as we become more in harmony with that Universe in our own mind, we can then conceive anything we really want or need - and will get the concept of what to do to make this come about.

7. All through our long written and verbal history, humankind has always believed in an invisible, infinite power - through which all was created and being continually re-created.

By whatever name you call it, the name doesn't matter - it works the same, regardless.

The objective is in the world around you, that which you see. The subjective consists of the spiritual and the impersonal.

Your conscious mind is the puzzle-solver, the place where you can decide, where you can figure things out, where you make your plans. Your subconscious mind, while it is impersonal and spiritual in nature, doesn't necessarily have that level of choice - but has connection to the Infinite's resources and brings results which we cannot understand or mimic.

However, your own will can harness the power of the subconscious - if you know how it is set up and works. And so, you can then utilize the unlimited potential of the Infinite. You just have to know and understand how these work.

8. The fascinating basis for the mind is that all your thinking is governed by one unchanging law.

Understanding and using this law means the world around you can now be exactly as you want it. This law holds the universe together in harmony, because without it - everything would be chaos and fall apart.

This is actually the secret to both good and evil.

Here's the explanation: What you think in your mind becomes action. If you think constructively, harmoniously, the results are good. Where you think negatively, destructively - the results are evil.

If you work with constructive thoughts in your mind, your life ends up with all the good you could possibly want. Where you are critical, negative, destructive - your life will have upset, bad accidents, problems.

When you work with this awhile, you'll see that we are to cease hating (as hate is simply destructive) and so learn exactly how when we quit "sowing with wind" with such destructive thought, opinion, and attitude - we then quit "reaping the whirlwind."

9. Here you can learn to make the tools to build or create any thing you want in your life.

In order to change conditions around you, you have to change yourself. Your world around you is the result of your past thinking.

Once you plant that seed in your mind, then the "law of growth" says it will ultimately bear the fruit you want. Hold that idea, consider that it already exists. Repeat this thought regularly and it comes about. By doing this, you change yourself - and by doing that, change the world around you.

Just as two things can't occupy the same place at the same time, if you let thoughts of fear or insecurity into your mind, you will stay fearful and insecure. Replace those thoughts with courage, power, self-reliance, and confidence.

A simple, natural, and easy way to do this is to adopt an affirmation that fits you. This positive thought can then start driving out the negative ones - and so invite the native joy within to surface. Your positive actions will then follow and give you the joyous results you seek.

10. Nothing happens without a definite cause. Once you understand the causes, you can create any effect, control any situation.

And as you achieve your inevitable success, you'll know exactly why and how it happened.

The ordinary person is governed by their feelings and emotions. And so their thoughts justify why they "feels" that way - or - they act like a puppet on a string to whatever emotion is present in their life at that moment. That ordinary, typical, average person never analyzes his problems back to their cause - because that person doesn't really consider that there is a cause for every effect. Just more effect. Such a person thinks only to justify their actions and what happens to them. Poor work production is some other reason, getting laid off or fired is always someone else's fault.

When you understand that there can't be an effect without a cause, you then can get down to what you are doing and thinking that started the ball rolling. You can then have all the friendship, love, and approval in your life that you want. A better job or a pay raise is working smarter, not just harder - but it's caused, not accidental or a lottery payout.

11. Every result, every effect in this universe is the result of a cause.

And that result, that effect then becomes cause to another effect, and so on. This universe is built on chains of events.

And all these event-chains still operate by immutable Universal laws. The law of attraction is one of these. Like attracts like. As you know this and put this into effect, you start a new chain of causation which has endless possibilities.

Where you disown what happens in your life, where you complain, you then will help bring into your life more chains of causation which cause you more conditions to complain about. Because you forgot to apply the law you know, to be the cause in order to create the effect you really want.

We are responsible for everything that happens around us - just to that exact degree.

12. This key statement is made in here: "*You must first have the knowledge of your power; second, the courage to dare; third, the faith to do.*"

Where you concentrate, giving thoughts your entire attention, you will then fill your mind with these and related, harmonious thoughts. And so begin the process of attracting like things to you.

Knowledge doesn't apply itself. You are responsible to act on what you know. So plant and fertilize the seed in your mind as a cause, a living purpose.

The point of concentration cannot be underestimated in its power. An out-of-focus image results from an out-of-focus camera. Get your own mental pictures sharp, distinct, clear - and the effects you want in your life will be just exactly as you thought them.

13. Just as physical science has created amazing inventions that have improved our quality of living, we are can now see the basics spiritual science - which has the capacity for routinely creating even more amazing effects in our lives.

Your dreams can make a new reality. And while this chapter goes into more detail, the sum of it is this: You have to conceive before you act, and you have to give before you get. The Universe, surrounding and being part of everything around us - then will respond through those chains of causation in kind.

14. To the exact degree you think creative and constructive thoughts - these start evolving into fact around you.

And your conscious thought so controls your subconscious.

We've found so far that thought is a spiritual activity and is creative in nature. Denial brings about more negative results, as you are not using creative thought when you deny.

However, as you quit negative thinking, the negative effects start to disappear. Those chains of effects, like the plant cut off at the roots, eventually wither and fade away.

This probably seems counter-intuitive. It isn't how we were taught in school, or how we learned from our fellow classmates how to act. But to the degree you concentrate on negative thought and actions, you get negative results. When you forward critical, discordant thought - you are forming the root for a new and critical, discordant effect to grow around you.

It's what you choose to concentrate on with your mind.

15. You are surrounded by a Universe which is everywhere, which records every thought placed in it, which has potential to create any effect. In short, omnipresent, omniscient, omnipotent.

You have already learned that to concentrate your mind on precise thoughts will create chains of effects that then result in what you originally concentrated on.

There are natural laws at work here. Where we exercise our body, we become stronger. Where we exercise our will and control the thoughts in our mind, we also become stronger. Putting our new strength to use at applying these natural laws brings more of what we want to us even faster. And to release our native happiness within, we just need to cooperate with and utilize these natural laws.

16. Wealth is an effect, not a cause. It only shows the value of what you've been doing and exchanging with others.

It is only a means to the end, not the end itself.

Sure, success often has wealth associated with it. But to get that wealth, you have to be successful, and to be successful, you have to get the concepts that go with that success in your mind.

As the thoughts you keep are creative and harmonious, this internal vision will create like effects on the world around you. To the exact degree you hold that vision, and make your actions harmonious with it - this is the exact degree it will start manifesting in your world.

And your visions are the result of your concentration - not just an undisciplined mind with a "wild imagination". Carefully develop and hold your own ideal scene in your mind - work this up, and then work from this - and see your works arrive around you.

17. As you consider, as you concentrate, you are developing an Ideal. The quality of this ideal determines the outcome you'll arrive at.

As you keep this ideal in your mind, you will start attracting similar thoughts which are harmonious to your creation. These are known as Intuition. As you continue to work with these concentrated thoughts, you will then get more solutions to the various aspects of that Ideal as you build it in your mind.

Learn to let these flow in, as you can now tap into the contained knowledge of the Universe around you - and build a much greater and higher Ideal than you had ever imagined before.

18. You can now consider that as no person is an island in this stream of living, we all are interconnected and interrelated.

You'll see by review, that we attract those around us just as we originally held those types of thought in our mind.

So the glue which holds this Universe together is the Law of Attraction. Hateful, destructive thoughts attract hateful people to you. Cheerful, optimistic, and creative thought will fill your world with those who are creatively optimistic. Destructive effects come early to those who consider these ideals only. Success, prosperity, good health - these come to those who concentrate on higher ideals.

We are all only following Natural laws. Your ability to use these laws depend first on your knowledge of them, and second on your persistent exercising them. Your ability to concentrate improves with your practice - just like any physical or mental skill. Practice makes perfect.

19. While fear, and other self-limiting thoughts, are able to paralyze the body into inaction - this is just a thought and usually transient.

The real power you have doesn't depend on any limiting thoughts, but draws from another source. While we do not have to understand this source at present in order to be, do, or have anything and everything we really want - you can know that it allows all of your success, if you follow the laws that govern it.

And beyond simply acquiring all the physical things of this world for our own use - we can transcend this mortal plane and "express the highest possible degree of mental, moral, and spiritual efficiency."

20. If God is everywhere and in everything, where is Evil, the Devil, and Hell?

Around you and encompassing every cell of your body is Life. By many names, this source has been observed in all its mysteries by every branch of science, every child, every aged philosopher. And while perhaps only the enlightened ever understood it in any real sense - it nevertheless cannot be argued that it doesn't exist.

By any name, it follows the same rules and laws we've already covered. There is no bad effect which isn't caused by a lack of good. You cannot shovel darkness out of a room, you just turn on or shine a light. And so are all negatives in this universe.

All you see around you is your own presence or lack of positive, creative thought. Everything.

So where you sit in quiet meditation or prayer, you tap into a line of thought called inspiration - which is just tapping into that broad, ever-present quantity of existence. Through this, you can find and connect with all the positive and creative source for everything around you.

As you work to align your thoughts with the harmony that already exists in the Universe, you tap into more and more of this latent power all around you.

21. As there are laws of the physical (gravity, for example) - there are also laws of the spiritual.

As you know and apply these laws, you tap into and channel a power much greater than any current idea of limitation you currently have.

Prayer and meditation use these laws. And successful results from these is simply knowing and applying those laws.

As you hold a thought in your mind (concentration), this is then impressed on the subconscious and so the laws of the Universe then bring it to actualization.

The bulk of the people currently on this planet do not know or understand what these spiritual laws are and how they work. So they live as paupers surrounded by riches. They only have to ask and anything will be given them. But they do not know how or that they can ask.

22. Your health is dependent on your thoughts - how you use your mind. Constant negative thinking produces adverse reactions on the body.

> *"The various forms of inflammation, paralysis, nervousness and diseased conditions generally, are the manifestation of fear, worry, care, anxiety, jealousy, hatred and similar thought."*

It's not the food you eat or the water you drink - but the residue left over which eventually poisons the body to any greater or lesser degree. This is retained because of residual destructive thought.

> *"The problem, then, before us in the healing of disease is to increase the inflow and distribution of vital energy throughout the system, and this can only be done by eliminating thoughts of fear, worry, care, anxiety, jealousy, hatred, and every other destructive thought, which tend to tear down and destroy the nerves and glands which control the excretion and elimination of poisonous and waste matter."*

While governments can decree that there are no "cures" outside of Medical Science - any adverse situation can be remarkably alleviated, if not eliminated, through changing any residual negative thought to positive. And making this consistent and continual in your life.

23. This chapter tells of the rules and laws which govern that fiction known as "Money".

Money is only a symbol which represents the valuable service you give to friends and those around you. To retain balance, the natural world is constantly seeking to flow back to any individual an equal return to the source.

In order to make a "money magnet" of yourself, you have to figure out how to first make money for other people. The great financiers are nothing but channels for the incredible wealth that already exists around each of us. They assist others with handling their money flows and benefit as result.

What you have already learned about your mind and the thoughts you use in it - these laws and principles govern how much wealth you create in the world around you. Your concentration on creative and constructive thought - and the inspired action you receive through your silent prayer and meditation - these create all the wealth and success you could ever imagine to want.

And the more this is preceded by open-handed giving - value given away without any thought of return - the more effective, abundant, and speedy that return.

24. As you've studied all of Haanel's lessons up to this point, and completed the practical assignments he set out with each chapter, all the very practical points of creating and fulfilling every possible need have been laid out for you.

Anything you actually want to be, do, have, acquire, or attain - all of these are now completely open to you:

> *"The fruit of this knowledge is, as it were, a gift of the Gods; it is the "truth" that makes men free, not only*

free from every lack and limitation, but free from sorrow, worry and care, and, is it not wonderful to realize that this law is no respector of persons, that it makes no difference what your habit of thought may be, the way has been prepared."

If you are of a religious sense, then any amount of inspiration is open to you. If you are philosophic, then this same inspiration will bring you any answers you seek. If you are of the scientific approach, then all manner and kind of solutions can show up for your use.

Practically, the entire world has just been opened up to you. You now know the laws which govern all life - how these work and how you can use them.

It is now up to you to put them to use. And create the world of your dreams around you.

- - - -

Our next author put all these ethereal concepts into pragmatic, tightly-worded reality - in a style the local farmers could easily understand. And these words still shake the worlds of his readers today...

Wallace Wattles - Give Value in Excess

Born to in Illinois to a gardener and house-keeper, and raised spending most of his life in Indiana, our earliest record of Wattles' life is that of a farm laborer – a hired hand. Probably the most "uneducated" of all the authors we cover here, he nevertheless was able to transition from a poor and austere background to a well-paid author and a comfortable existence for himself and his family by the time he died at age 51.

Lacking academic papers didn't stop him from studying everything he could in the areas of self-help and personal development. Visiting nearby Chicago, he attended various lectures and communed with New Thought authors and publishers. He was known to have studied Hegel and Emerson as well as other authors who are included under the wide New Thought umbrella.

Also consistent with our other authors is that he lived what he wrote. And would test out his own theories before he wrote about them. But as he wrote, he only told people to test his writings in their own lives, not to take his word as an authority.

Wallace Wattles published the "Science of Getting Rich" as one of his last books in the year he died. And interestingly, a worn xeroxed copy of that book - with the last pages missing - was handed to television producer Rhonda Byrne by her daughter. This book was credited as being the inspiration for "The Secret" DVD.

As we continue through this book, you start seeing various datums reinforced by these authors - which is the basic premise of my "Go Thunk Yourself!" studies - that there is one, common, underlying system of laws and principles which govern all self-help and personal development.

And as Wattles summized, this can make a person rich - and can also bring *anything* that person wants into their lives by the same token. He wrote this in a style and manner such that even the miners in his home town would be able to easily read and understand these basics.

As we continue through this book, you start seeing various datums reinforced by these authors - which is the basic premise of "Go Thunk Yourself!" - that there is one, common, underlying system of laws and principles which govern all self-help and personal development.

With this book, we are taking a slightly different approach. Namely that you already have and know everything you need to make your life a success. You only have to uncover all that knowledge. Then every good thing you've always been able to have will start showing up around you.

In this chapter, we see that what Wattles covers stays true to our central concept: all the Freedom, Happiness and Peace *already* lies within you. While many have held that his book is a path all on it's own, I've found that he really just tells you some very non-inclusive principles which can be added to any other belief system - or vice versa.

Even today as I write this, I find in reviewing him that his Summary covers all the key points Wattles wanted to make from his book. In conjunction with Hill, and Haanel, you can see exactly why this book continues to be passed around, shared, and sold nearly 100 years later.

Looking over his work in that light, it has a whole new flavor. Again, don't take this essay as a gospel understanding to swallow wholesale. Rather, use what you can and what makes sense to you. Refer to the original book as you need to, if more clarification is needed:

> *"THERE IS A THINKING STUFF FROM WHICH ALL THINGS ARE MADE, and which, in its original state, permeates, penetrates, and fills the inter-spaces of the universe."*

> *A thought in this substance produces the thing that is imaged by the thought.*

A person can form things in his thought, and by impressing his thought upon formless substance can cause the thing he thinks about to be created.

Here is the underlying basic to this book. This aligns with our three earlier authors completely. You are in control over your own life and whatever you want to do with it. You can think in your mind whatever you want. And from this, all you want shows up around you.

In order to do this, a person must pass from the competitive to the creative mind. Otherwise he cannot be in harmony with formless intelligence, which is always creative and never competitive in spirit.

This point of creative vs. competitive can't be understated. Competition is a fiction, practically. Look it over and you'll find that competition has to be created. Whether it is on a "level playing field" of sports, or the unequal struggle of similar companies offering similar products to a shared public. But to "compete" by offering nearly identical products to the same people is to give up the idea that you can create something different. And so the idea of commodity markets.

A person may come into full harmony with the formless substance by entertaining a lively and sincere gratitude for the blessings it bestows upon him. Gratitude unifies the mind of man with the intelligence of substance, so that man's thoughts are received by the formless. A person can remain upon the creative plane only by uniting himself with the formless intelligence through a deep and continuous feeling of gratitude.

The idea of achieving a "full harmony" in your life is a key point. And here is the idea of gratitude, which keeps you "in tune" with the Universal, so you can know your own Freedom, Happiness, and Peace. This is also "the Zone" which people strive to get into and stay in.

*A person must form a clear and definite mental
image of the things he wishes to have, to do, or to
become, and he must hold this mental image in his
thoughts, while being deeply grateful to the supreme
that all his desires are granted to him. The person
who wishes to get rich must spend his leisure hours in
contemplating his vision, and in earnest
thanksgiving that the reality is being given to him.
Too much stress cannot be laid on the importance of
frequent contemplation of the mental image, coupled
with unwavering faith and devout gratitude. This is
the process by which the impression is given to the
formless and the creative forces set in motion.*

Here the certainty of your own ideals, goals, and purposes show
up again. Holding these in a concentrated effort or approach to
life, along with the gratitude of thanksgiving that you already
have it, then aligns your life. What you concentrate on then
shows up around you. It's much wider than just getting rich -
it's getting all the Freedom, Happiness, and Peace you could
ever ask for and more.

*The creative energy works through the established
channels of natural growth, and of the industrial and
social order. All that is included in his mental image
will surely be brought to the person who follows the
instructions given above, and whose faith does not
waver. What he wants will come to him through the
ways of established trade and commerce.*

The world around us is simply the composite of all of our
thoughts put together. It's no more mysterious or cause-effect
induced than that. It's not this big materialistically-organized
complex of stuff which is overpowering and cannot be
controlled or managed by any one person. It is just the
composite of all our past thinking assembled in one place.

So any thought in this area brings about the manifestation
through these "ways of established trade and commerce."
Because miracles are one thing, but when most people don't

"believe" in them, the next fall-back is to have whatever you really conceive and concentrate on to come from the "real world" around us.

> *In order to receive his own when it is ready to come to him, a person must be in action in a way that causes him to more than fill his present place. He must keep in mind the purpose to get rich through realization of his mental image. And he must do, every day, all that can be done that day, taking care to do each act in a successful manner. He must give to every person a use value in excess of the cash value he receives, so that each transaction makes for more life, and he must hold the advancing thought so that the impression of increase will be communicated to all with whom he comes into contact.*

This is the key to the entire book, Wattle's philosophy summed up in a single paragraph. The real successes which have been created with the Golden Rule are built on this one point: that when you work for others and get across to them that when they work in abundance for others, this is the exact way abundance shows up for themselves.

To the exact degree we act on this single concept, that we actually get the bulk of everyone we come into contact with into this same idea of natural abundance, it will be just to that degree which we meet with success in our own lives. Period.

While abundance is a necessary concept to spread to others so that both they and you can get rich, imagine the concept being spread about being Happy all the time. Or the idea that anyone can be and use all the Freedom they want. Or even the idea that Peace is internally generated (we don't have to wait around for governments to act) and so spread Peace through out the world by everyone being internally at peace with themselves...

> *The men and women who practice the foregoing instructions will certainly get rich, and the riches they receive will be in exact proportion to the definiteness of their vision, the fixity of their purpose,*

the steadiness of their faith, and the depth of their gratitude.

Boil this all down, and you get to the same ideas which Hill, and Haanel (plus the other authors later in this book) all hold as vital:

To the extent that you consider you *can* change and control what you think and what you would like to have show up around you - it is exactly to *that* extent, plus your faith in *yourself*, that your world will change.

So, if you haven't guessed already, it's entirely up to you to change the world you live in.

- - - -

But I don't mean to get really "heavy" and serious here. We still have some other authors with different viewpoints to review. And these have a lot to say about how you can live a life that from your native calmness and cheerful expectancy about all the great things coming your way.

Earl Nightingale - Know The Strangest Secret

Born in Los Angeles and raised in Long Beach during the Depression years, the poverty Earl Nightingale's family endured sparked his years of study to find out why and "how come" his family and relatives were poor while others were much better off. And his introduction to the Long Beach City library during his childhood started fulfilling that quest. (Interestingly, many of these public libraries were started with Carnegie grants...)

Wanting to see the world, Nightingale joined the US Marines and got as far as Hawaii when the Japanese struck Pearl Harbor. He was one of the 12 surviving Marines on board the Arizona that day. He volunteered at the local radio station while stationed in Hawaii, but his professional work in this field began in Phoenix, where he learned his basics and went on to Chicago's WGN to build a profitable and expanding daily commentary program. While so successful that he retired from his union broadcasting job at age 35, during this he also uncovered a key secret in a used book store in Chicago – the secret he had been looking for his entire life – found in a used copy of Napoleon Hill's "Think and Grow Rich".

Owning an insurance company, he would often spend hours speaking to and motivating his sales force. When due for a long vacation, his sales manager suggested he record a talk they could play over and over in his absence. Waking with inspiration at 4am one morning, he rushed to his study to write out what had come to him during his sleep. This recording became the first spoken-word record to sell over a million copies and go "Gold".

And that success led him to partner with Lloyd Conant to form Nightingale-Conant corporation, the first organization devoted to self-help recordings. At the same time, Nightingale's radio program, "Our Changing World" was quickly becoming more popular. Ultimately, it became the most syndicated radio program of its time, and was heard in the US, the Armed Forced Network, and 23 countries overseas.

While I listened to Nightingale's popular weekly radio show, "Our Changing World" as a youngster growing up, but never knew that his worldwide popularity was started by a single recorded album.

Long after writing "Go Thunk Yourself!", I stumbled across this classic. It actually tells the whole story that you see in that super-long treatise that Haanel wrote.

Yet he spoke this in the very modern way we can all understand. And in the writing, you miss a good deal of the content given in the original spoken-voice recording.

The key point here is to see Nightingale's view of what we've already covered. Because the view he gives is novel and his own path up the Mountain – which had brought him his own riches and success by the time he had authored this recording. And then he sat out on yet another amazing career.

I give this here as anyone can stumble onto these data – just as Hill, Wattles, Haanel, and Nightingale have. Look over this transcript – and get the recording if you can (it's a free download on the Internet as well as still being available from Nightingale-Conant) – so you can get your own message from this as you seek the Freedom within you.

THE STRANGEST SECRET

Know what will happen to 100 individuals who start even at the age of 25, and who believe they will be successful? By the age of 65, only five out of 100 will make the grade! Why do so many fail? What happened to the sparkle that was there when they were 25? What became of their dreams, their hopes, their plans ... and why is there such a large disparity between what theses people intended to do and what they actually accomplished?

Some years ago, the late Nobel prize-winning Dr. Albert Schweitzer was asked by a reporter, "Doctor, what's wrong with men today?; The great doctor was silent a moment, and then he said, "Men simply don't think!"

It's about this that I want to talk with you. We live today in a golden age. This is an era that humanity has looked forward to, dreamed of, and worked toward for thousands of years. We live in the richest era that ever existed on the face of the earth ... a land of abundant opportunity for everyone.

However, if you take 100 individuals who start even at the age of 25, do you have any idea what will happen to those men and women by the time they're 65? These 100 people believe they're going to be successful. They are eager toward life, there is a certain sparkle in their eye, an erectness to their carriage, and life seems like a pretty interesting adventure to them.

But by the time they're 65, only one will be rich, four will be financially independent, five will still be working, and 54 will be broke -depending on others for life's necessities.

Only five out of 100 make the grade! Why do so many fail? What has happened to the sparkle that was there when they were 25? What has become of the dreams, the hopes, the plans ... and why is there such a large disparity between what these people intended to do and what they actually accomplished?

THE DEFINITION OF SUCCESS

First, we have to define success and here is the best definition I've ever been able to find: "Success is the progressive realization of a worthy ideal."

A success is the school teacher who is teaching because that's what he or she wants to do. A success is the entrepreneur who start his own company because that was his dream - that's what he wanted to do.

A success is the salesperson who wants to become the best salesperson in his or her company and sets forth on the pursuit of that goal.

A success is anyone who is realizing a worthy predetermined ideal, because that's what he or she decided to do ... deliberately. But only one out of 20 does that! The rest are "failures." Rollo May, the distinguished psychiatrist, wrote a wonderful book called Man's Search for Himself, and in this book he says: "The opposite of courage in our society is not cowardice ... it is conformity." And there you have the reason for so many failures. Conformity - people acting like everyone else, without knowing why or where they are going.

We learn to read by the time we're seven. We learn to make a living by the time we're 30. Often by that time we're not only making a living, we're supporting a family. And yet by the time we're 65, we haven't learned how to become financially independent in the richest land that has ever been known. Why? We conform! Most of us are acting like the wrong percentage group - the 95 who don't succeed.

GOALS

Have you ever wondered why so many people work so hard and honestly without ever achieving anything in particular, and why others don't seem to work hard, yet seem to get everything? They seem to have the "magic touch." You've heard people say, "Everything he touches turns to gold." Have you ever noticed that a person who becomes successful tends to continue to become more successful? And, on the other hand, have you noticed how someone who's a failure tends to continue to fail?

The difference is goals. People with goals succeed because they know where they're going. It's that simple. Failures, on the other hand, believe that their lives are shaped by circumstances ... by things that happen to them ... by exterior forces.

Think of a ship with the complete voyage mapped out and planned. The captain and crew know exactly where the ship is going and how long it will take - it has a definite goal. And 9,999 times out of 10,000, it will get there.

Now let's take another ship - just like the first - only let's not put a crew on it, or a captain at the helm. Let's give it no aiming point, no goal, and no destination. We just start the engines and let it go. I think you'll agree that if it gets out of the harbor at all, it will either sink or wind up on some deserted beach - a derelict. It can't go anyplace because it has no destination and no guidance.

It's the same with a human being. However, the human race is fixed, not to prevent the strong from winning, but to prevent the weak from losing. Society today can be likened to a convoy in time of war. The entire society is slowed down to protect its weakest link, just as the naval convoy has to go at the speed that will permit its slowest vessel to remain in formation.

That's why it's so easy to make a living today. It takes no particular brains or talent to make a living and support a family today. We have a plateau of so-called "security." So, to succeed, all we must do is decide how high above this plateau we want to aim.

Throughout history, the great wise men and teachers, philosophers, and prophets have disagreed with one another on many different things. It is only on this one point that they are in complete and unanimous agreement - the key to success and the key to failure is this:

WE BECOME WHAT WE THINK ABOUT

This is The Strangest Secret! Now, why do I say it's strange, and why do I call it a secret? Actually, it isn't a secret at all. It was first promulgated by some of the earliest wise men, and it appears again and again throughout the Bible. But very few people have learned it or understand it. That's why it's strange, and why for some equally strange reason it virtually remains a secret.

Marcus Aurelius, the great Roman Emperor, said:

> *"A man's life is what his thoughts make of it."*

Disraeli said this:

> *"Everything comes if a man will only wait ... a human being with a settled purpose must accomplish it, and nothing can resist a will that will stake even existence for its fulfillment."*

William James said:

> *"We need only in cold blood act as if the thing in question were real, and it will become infallibly real by growing into such a connection with our life that it will become real. It will become so knit with habit and emotion that our interests in it will be those which characterize belief." He continues, " ... only you must, then, really wish these things, and wish them exclusively, and not wish at the same time a hundred other incompatible things just as strongly."*

My old friend Dr. Norman Vincent Peale put it this way:

> *"If you think in negative terms, you will get negative results. If you think in positive terms, you will achieve positive results." George Bernard Shaw said: "People are always blaming their circumstances for what they are. I don't believe in circumstances. The people who get on in this world are the people who get up and look for the circumstances they want, and if they can't find them, make them."*

Well, it's pretty apparent, isn't it? We become what we think about. A person who is thinking about a concrete and worthwhile goal is going to reach it, because that's what he's thinking about. Conversely, the person who has no goal, who doesn't know where he's going, and whose thoughts must therefore be thoughts of confusion, anxiety, fear, and worry will thereby create a life of frustration, fear, anxiety and worry.

And if he thinks about nothing ... he becomes nothing.

AS YE SOW - SO SHALL YE REAP

The human mind is much like a farmer's land. The land gives the farmer a choice. He may plant in that land whatever he chooses. The land doesn't care what is planted. It's up to the farmer to make the decision. The mind, like the land, will return what you plant, but it doesn't care what you plant. If the farmer plants two seeds - one a seed of corn, the other nightshade, a deadly poison, waters and takes care of the land, what will happen?

Remember, the land doesn't care. It will return poison in just as wonderful abundance as it will corn. So up come the two plants - one corn, one poison as it's written in the Bible, "As ye sow, so shall ye reap." The human mind is far more fertile, far more incredible and mysterious than the land, but it works the same way. It doesn't care what we plant ... success ... or failure. A concrete, worthwhile goal ... or confusion, misunderstanding, fear, anxiety, and so on. But what we plant it must return to us.

The problem is that our mind comes as standard equipment at birth. It's free. And things that are given to us for nothing, we place little value on. Things that we pay money for, we value.

The paradox is that exactly the reverse is true. Everything that's really worthwhile in life came to us free - our minds, our souls, our bodies, our hopes, our dreams, our ambitions, our intelligence, our love of family and children and friends and country. All these priceless possessions are free.

But the things that cost us money are actually very cheap and can be replaced at any time. A good man can be completely wiped out and make another fortune. He can do that several times. Even if our home burns down, we can rebuild it. But the things we got for nothing, we can never replace.

Our mind can do any kind of job we assign to it, but generally speaking, we use it for little jobs instead of big ones. So decide now.

What is it you want? Plant your goal in your mind. It's the most important decision you'll ever make in your entire life.

Do you want to excel at your particular job? Do you want to go places in your company ... in your community? Do you want to get rich? All you have got to do is plant that seed in your mind, care for it, work steadily toward your goal, and it will become a reality.

It not only will, there's no way that it cannot. You see, that's a law - like the laws of Sir Isaac Newton, the laws of gravity. If you get on top of a building and jump off, you'll always go down - you'll never go up.

And it's the same with all the other laws of nature. They always work. They're inflexible. Think about your goal in a relaxed, positive way.

Picture yourself in your mind's eye as having already achieved this goal.

See yourself doing the things you will be doing when you have reached your goal.

Every one of us is the sum total of our own thoughts. We are where we are because that's exactly where we really want or feel we deserve to be - whether we'll admit that or not. Each of us must live off the fruit of our thoughts in the future, because what you think today and tomorrow - next month and next year - will mold your life and determine your future. You're guided by your mind.

I remember one time I was driving through eastern Arizona and I saw one of those giant earth-moving machines roaring along the road with what looked like 30 tons of dirt in it - a tremendous, incredible machine - and there was a little man perched way up on top with the wheel in his hands, guiding it. As I drove along I was struck by the similarity of that machine to the human mind. Just suppose you're sitting at the controls of such a vast source of energy. Are you going to sit back and fold your arms and let it run itself into a ditch? Or are you going to keep both hands firmly on the wheel and control and direct this power to a specific, worthwhile purpose? It's up to you. You're in the driver's seat.

You see, the very law that gives us success is a double-edged sword. We must control our thinking. The same rule that can lead people to lives of success, wealth, happiness, and all the things they ever dreamed of - that very same law can lead them into the gutter. It's all in how they use it ... for good or for bad. That is The Strangest Secret! Do what the experts since the dawn of recorded history have told us to do: pay the price, by becoming the person you want to become. It's not nearly as difficult as living unsuccessfully.

The moment you decide on a goal to work toward, you're immediately a successful person - you are then in that rare group of people who know where they're going. Out of every hundred people, you belong to the top five. Don't concern yourself too much with how you are going to achieve your goal - leave that completely to a power greater than yourself. All you have to do is know where you're going. The answers will come to you of their own accord, and at the right time.

30-DAY ACTION PLAN -

FOR PUTTING THE STRANGEST SECRET TO WORK FOR YOU

For the next 30-days follow each of these steps every day until you have achieved your goal.

1. Write on a card what it is you want more that anything else. It may be more money. Perhaps you'd like to double your income or make a specific amount of money. It may be a beautiful home. It may be success at your job. It may be a particular position in life. It could be a more harmonious family.

Write down on your card specifically what it is you want. Make sure it's a single goal and clearly defined. You needn't show it to anyone, but carry it with you so that you can look at it several times a day. Think about it in a cheerful, relaxed, positive way each morning when you get up, and immediately you have something to work for - something to get out of bed for, something to live for.

2. Look at it every chance you get during the day and just before going to bed at night. As you look at it, remember that you must become what you think about, and since you're thinking about your goal, you realize that soon it will be yours. In fact, it's really yours the moment you write it down and begin to think about it.

3. Stop thinking about what it is you fear. Each time a fearful or negative thought comes into your mind, replace it with a mental picture of your positive and worthwhile goal. And there will come a time when you'll feel like giving up. It's easier for a human being to think negatively than positively. That's why only five percent are successful! You must begin now to place yourself in that group.

4. "Act as though it were impossible to fail," as Dorothea Brande said. No matter what your goal - if you've kept your goal before you every day - you'll wonder and marvel at this new life you've found.

5. Your success will always be measured by the quality and quantity of service you render. Most people will tell you that they want to make money, without understanding this law. The only people who make money work in a mint. The rest of us must earn money. This is what causes those who keep looking for something for nothing, or a free ride, to fail in life. Success is not the result of making money; earning money is the result of success - and success is in direct proportion to our service.

Most people have this law backwards. It's like the man who stands in front of the stove and says to it: "Give me heat and then I'll add the wood." How many men and women do you know, or do you suppose there are today, who take the same attitude toward life? There are millions.

We've got to put the fuel in before we can expect heat. Likewise, we've got to be of service first before we can expect money. Don't concern yourself with the money. Be of service ... build ... work ... dream ... create! Do this and you'll find there is no limit to the prosperity and abundance that will come to you.

6. Don't start your test until you've made up your mind to stick with it. If you should fail during your first 30 days - by that I mean suddenly find yourself overwhelmed by negative thoughts -simply start over again from that point and go 30 more days. Gradually, your new habit will form, until you find yourself one of that wonderful minority to whom virtually nothing is impossible.

7. Above all ... don't worry! Worry brings fear, and fear is crippling. The only thing that can cause you to worry during your test is trying to do it all yourself. Know that all you have to do is hold your goal before you; everything else will take care of itself.

Take this 30-day test, then repeat it ... then repeat it again. Each time it will become more a part of you until you'll wonder how you could have ever have lived any other way. Live this new way and the floodgates of abundance will open and pour over you more riches than you may have dreamed existed. Money? Yes, lots of it. But what's more important, you'll have peace ... you'll be in that wonderful minority who lead calm, cheerful, successful lives.

Start today. You have nothing to lose -but you have your whole life to win.

Serge Kahili King - Live Lessons from Long Ago

Serge Kahili King's training began with his father, who was assigned by the British Diplomatic Corps to Hawaii in 1911. Owing to a unique mystical experience, the elder King met and was adopted by an Hawaiian family. They trained King's father in an ancient tradition of Hawaiian shamanism.

At 14, Serge began his training under his father in these ways, but his father died within 3 years of his starting. Fortunately, Serge was adopted by the Kahili family as a grandson. He started traditional education with his uncle which continued for many years, interspersed with college degrees (a Bachelor's in Asiatic Studies in Colorado, a Master's in International Management in Arizona, and a Doctorate of Psychology in California). Interspersed with this formal Western training was spending 7 years studying under an West African shaman while also participating in humanitarian programs as part of the Catholic Relief Services.

King's uncle continued working with his nephew until, as Serge tells it, "... I was training with my uncle at that time and finally decided that this knowledge, based on what I had learned from them, based on Africa, and based on what I knew of the world situation, this knowledge was too precious not to share." The result of this was the organization Aloha International, which has as its purpose the dissemination of Hawaiian traditions and the wide knowledge Dr. King has accumulated.

Since the point where he realized that all the truth he needed to know was already his for the asking, he has been working to help other people find that truth which lies within themselves.

It is just our fortune that he is also an accomplished writer and speaker, having produced more books, videos, seminars, recordings, and other published works on the subject of Huna than any other known author in history.

I bring this short lecture to you to tell you of the incredible historic basis of these principles you are studying – and as well to brief you on the 7 basic principles which explain not only how this Universe works – that entire 24-lesson Hannel study, as well as that 16-volume "Law of Success" which Hill authored.

These 7 principles also explain how immutable Laws like the Golden Rule and the Law of Attraction work.

Again, like any of these authors – you could study King and Huna for the rest of this life and use that as a path almost solely to regain your own Freedom, Happiness, and Joy from here on out. So open your heart to understand these truths as you set your mind aside.

THE HUNA PRINCIPLES

Serge Kahili King speaking from Kauai

Aloha! Greetings to you, and to this ocean and to this land, to this wind and to this sky! I want to share with you a part of the Hawaiian cultural heritage.

A very long time ago in the islands of the Pacific, there were wise men and women who looked at the world, who observed the patterns of nature, the behavior of animals and plants, human beings, and they came to some conclusions about life, about what life is all about, about how life works. And they gave a name to this knowledge. They called it Huna, Ka Huna, the secret, the inner knowledge, the hidden knowledge.

And from this knowledge they developed seven ideas, seven principles, and these are what I want to share with you. The people who did this, who practiced this knowledge, were called Kapua; nowadays we might call them Shaman. And they had a very special way of looking at life, of seeing.

1. **IKE** - our ideas create our reality.

2. **KALA** - there are no limits.

3. **MAKIA** --energy flows where attention goes.

4. **MANAWA** - now is the moment of power.

5. **ALOHA** - to love is to be happy with.

6. **MANA** - all power comes from within.

7. **PONO** - effectiveness is the measure of truth.

Now the first of these ideas in Hawaiian is called **IKE** (ee-kay). And the idea in English is **The world is what you think it is**. This life of ours is a dream, our dream, a dream that we share with other people, that we share with the earth; a dream that we also share with ourselves alone. It's a way of saying that this dream of our experience, this reality as we call it, comes from inside, comes from our thoughts, our ideas, our beliefs, our fears, our desires, our angers and our pleasures. That all of the ways that we think produces this experience of ours. That from night comes day, from thought comes reality.

If we would change this reality, says this knowledge, this philosophy if you will, if we would change this reality, then we must change ourselves. And it is wasted energy to try to change the outer world alone, but if we would truly change the outer world we must go within and find that place within us which is creating the outer world, and change that. Change that idea, change that fear to hope, change that anger to love, change that belief in lack to a belief in abundance. This is IKE, working from within to create the outer.

This is the most important of the ideas, and all of these ideas that we're going to talk about now come from this first one.

The next principle that comes from the first one is **KALA**. Kala, which says, **There are no limits**. Meaning that we are all connected. Each one of us is connected, mind and body, spirit and man, earth and plants and animals and clouds and sky and ocean. We are all one, we are all connected together.

Now Kala also says that separation is an illusion, but that because we can create our own reality with our thoughts, we sometimes create a sense, a belief in separation. And that as we believe we are separate, we create sickness. When the mind is separate from the body, when we think these two are separate, then in that way we create sickness. When the body, our body, ourselves are separate from the people around us, when we create that kind of separation in our thoughts and our feelings, then there is sickness in our relationships. When we feel we are separate from the earth, that the earth is a thing outside of us, then we get sick, and so does the earth. But Kala says that there is really, underneath all of that sense of separation, a real oneness. And that if we can get rid of those ideas and feelings and acts and behaviors and thoughts of separation, that oneness comes together. That connection is made again, we become healthy and whole within ourselves and with the world around us. This is Kala -- it is a way of creating that connection again, a freeing up.

You've probably seen in Hawaii, a gesture they do which says, 'Hang Loose!' And the meaning is very clear, it means that when you get uptight, when you create tension, then you create separation. So when you hang loose, when you relax, when you allow things to flow, you are healthier, relationships with everything are better, and a very interesting thing happens. When you are relaxed and flowing with things, it is easier to change them. So Kala is not saying that you must accept things the way they are, forever, without changing; it says that when you relax with them, you can change them easier. That's Kala.

The third idea that these wise people discovered was called **MAKIA** (mah-kee-ah). Makia, that **Energy flows where attention goes**. Wherever there is a flow of energy and attention, events are created. And wherever you direct your attention, and keep it directed in that way, to an object or to an idea, then the flow of energy carries. And according to the nature of your thoughts, that's the return flow that you get. So that if you're putting out and thinking very positive thoughts about the world around you, then positive energy flows back. And that when you are putting out and thinking negative thoughts about the world around you, then negative energy flows back, negative results come into your life. If you are putting our thoughts of abundance, and keeping that consistently, not just once in a while, but thinking that way, then abundance flows into your life. If you are thinking thoughts of happiness and joy, consistently, then to that degree happiness and joy flow back into your life. And where you focus on fear and anger, then you have fear and anger in your life. Where you focus on violence and upsetting and illness, then violence and upsetting and illness flow into your life.

You have the ability, the wonderful skill, says this knowledge, of deciding how you are going to focus your thoughts, your energy, your attention, and thereby change what is flowing back into your life. So all of these principles of this knowledge, starting from the first one, are telling you how to make the changes from within that will make the changes from outside.

There is a fourth idea, called **MANAWA** (man-ah-wah). Manawa is the idea that **Now is the moment of power**. This moment, right here. That there is no power in the past, no power in the future. That the past has no power over you either. That you are the one that has power right in this moment to change what you think, and then the past, and the effects of the past, fail to hold you. You walk forward in life from moment to moment with ideas about yourself and about the past. And it is those ideas, in every given moment,   that create your reality. If there is beauty in your life, as we have beauty in these Hawaiian Islands, then you are creating that beauty now. Says this idea, you increase that beauty by enjoying and appreciating that beauty now. If you stop appreciating that beauty, if you start losing your sense of beauty, then so does the land around you lose its beauty, as we have seen happens some places on this earth of ours. But the more you appreciate, take pleasure in the moment, the more you strengthen that, the more you increase that.

So it is not what you've been, but what you are, that makes what you have in any given moment. And the future, as well, does not lie in front of you, waiting for you to move forward and bump into it. The future is created in every present moment by the seeds of thought that you plant now. Sometimes we have weeds from the past, but we can pull those up now, and plant new seeds, and create a new future. So says this knowledge. As we go along, new seeds are planted, and if we decide that we don't like, at some moment, what these seeds have produced, then at any time, we can pull them up and plant new seeds. So it is every moment that we have our power, and there is power in everything else too, in every present moment.

One of the most wonderful ideas of this knowledge comes in a word that you've already heard, which is **ALOHA**. Aloha, which is so often taken to mean hello and good-bye. And it is used that way. We speak of the spirit of aloha which is so often taken to mean friendship. And it is friendship. But it is more. More than friendship, more than hello and good-bye, Aloha means love. Pure and simple, this is the meaning of that beautiful word. Love.

And even deeper within the word is the meaning of love, which is **To be happy with**. To be happy with something or someone, this is the great discovery, the most marvelous secret of this knowledge that was discovered by these people. That to love is to be happy with. To the degree that you are happy with yourself, with other people, with the world around you, you are in love. And love is being expressed, and love is flowing. But to the degree that you are criticizing, to the degree that you have anger, are not pleased with, do not like things in people around you, you reduce and diminish love. So that love has nothing to do with pain. Love has nothing to do with hurting people or being hurt. Love is the happiness in any relationship. Love is the happiness and the joy and the friendship and the pleasure in any relationship. Because to love is to be happy with.

The sixth principle is **MANA**. Mana is a word that has been often misunderstood, taken to mean energy alone. But Mana is an idea that means power, divine power, creative power. The concept of Mana is that there is once source of all power, and that source flows through each one of us. Not only us as human beings, but through the earth itself, through every stone, through every tree, through every cloud. Mana is the inner power that give every thing its own creativity. Mana is the power of the waves, of the sea to come up and kiss the shore. Mana is the power of the wind to carry the clouds and the birds, and blow across the lands and the ocean. Mana is the power of a stone to be strong and and stable. Mana is the power of human beings to be creative, in their own unique way. Mana is that source of power within each person, within each thing in this universe.

Now, most important from this comes the further idea that **All power comes from within**. This is the principle, meaning that there is no power outside of you that has any power over you. That all the power for your existence comes from that one source through you. That whenever we think that something else has power, whether it is nature, or whether it is another person, whether it is spirit, whatever it is that we think has more power over our lives than we do, all we are doing, according to this knowledge, is diminishing our own power, holding it back, holding it down. And in a very strange way pretending not to have the power we really have.

Now Mana is a power to do something, to be creative, not a power over. So it is that inner power within each thing, within each person to be itself, and to be itself to its utmost potential. Now the more we allow ourselves to experience that power, to feel it, to use it, to claim it, then we have that power to make ourselves match our highest potential.

There is a seventh principle, called **PONO**, and it says that **Effectiveness is the of truth**. That there is always another way to do anything. That we are never really stuck in one way, that there is no one way for anything. That there is no one truth, that there is no one method, one technique, one kind of medicine, one way to heal, one way to be happy, that there is only one person with whom you can be happy. There are many, many ways to achieve your goals, to be happy, to enjoy life, to fulfill it. This is Pono. That there is always another way to do anything.

The idea continues with the idea that plans are not sacred. Your purpose might be sacred, but the way you achieve that purpose is not. If you want to achieve a given purpose, however, you must use the means suitable to that purpose. If you want to create peace, then you must create peaceful means. For you will never get peace with violence. From violence you will only get more violence, until someday people may tire of the violence and get together and use peaceful means to create peace. But if you start out with peace in your heart, with a love of peace, says this knowledge, then you will move toward peace in your life. A very, very practical truth this one is. A very practical way of living, with yourself, and with other people.

These are the principles of this knowledge. Practiced by the Kapua, this knowledge called Kahuna, this knowledge that comes from these islands and others like them in the Pacific. Here is wisdom to share. And if you would share this, if you would use this, take any part of it that you choose, that you like, and apply and use it in your own life.

This is the end of my story. May you be blessed with peace and love, power and wisdom. Aloha!

"From the faraway, nearby." - Georgia O'Keefe

Part II - Releasing Your Freedom Essays

Section I - Getting Started

An Introduction to Lester Levenson's Releasing Technique

By this time, you've covered a great deal of materials. And I've given you more paths to choose from than you can count bees leaving to bring pollen back to their hive on a bright spring day.

We've already covered the fact that all the Freedom, Happiness, and Joy you could ever want is already within. And that these several authors above each laid out a path to make these your own in the Now, to let your own light shine.

I included all these classics I've been studying them for years, plus all the authors they mentioned. I even took up Bible studies I'd left in my youth in order to study engineering and computer texts. These few books I narrowed down to be my own chosen "path up the mountain." But like those college textbooks, there was always something missing for me (again, as I'll say over and over, disregard the man behind the curtain – don't accept anything I'm saying a gospel truth. Find out if it's true for you.)

While many had raved about Haanel's Master Key System, and Napoleon Hill had miles of testimonials, and the Bible was showing more people than ever how to let the Holy Spirit back into their life – but for me, something was still missing.

Then a friend sent me a copy of the Levenson releasing technique one day. It intrigued me. I sent off for more CD's while I also ransacked the Internet for everything I could find by it's discoverer, Lester Levenson.

When I got through this material several times (these recordings are mercifully short, and there are only a handful of actual texts) – I found that I had an explanation for something which had changed my life, but I had never fully understood.

Years before I started on the studies which resulted in my "Go Thunk Yourself" series, I was still working for a major West Coast corporation as a personal counselor, but was taking a vacation to the family farm. Life in those days was tough and hard-scrabble. No real way to get ahead and keep what you made.

I never expected to find a complete change to my life on a sunny, Midwestern summer day.

It was something straight out of Thoreau – or his mentor, Emerson. While on a walk in the woods, accompanied only by the two family dogs, I was suddenly struck by a profoundly immense Peace. All thought dropped away. For an unmeasured time, I was struck by the quiet of the woods – even though the birds were chirping, and insects buzzing, while the leaves whispered in the breeze – my mind was absolutely still and I was completely calm and at peace with the world and universe.

This "accidental" result was so moving, so life-changing that I wasn't able to continue my long career in Los Angeles after that. All my life's work in counseling others hadn't prepared me one bit for what I had just experienced. So I quit that 20-year career and moved back to Missouri in order to study and understand what I had experienced that day in the woods.

The answers didn't come easy – I still had to make a living – so my research was very part-time. I even went to college and got a few degrees in order to study what the world considered a "well-rounded education" consisted of.

The original "Go Thunk Yourself" was an early step, as well as finding, editing, and republishing a few dozen self-help and philosophic classics as a method of studying their contents. I generally had it licked, all figured out. I had a road map taped out and ready to follow – but I still didn't have an answer for what I had experienced that day.

Until I was introduced to the Lester Levenson and his releasing techniques.

Here, Levenson described what was originally just a two-step process to quiet the mind – and reproduce in anyone the exact phenomenon I had experienced.

And such phenomenon isn't rare. I've seen it in several authors, and read in biographies and legends of that type of scene appearing and happening to people all through history – in every continent on this planet.

But no one had explained it before, or given tools to reproduce it that *anyone* could actually use – anyone at all. No special training, no special equipment, no riches had to be paid out in installments in order to learn how.

My path, for me at least, was now mapped out. I don't have to search any more. Everything has stared to line up and make sense. The most practical point is that everything has gotten much simpler – which is the way things go when you are on a right path (to my experience, anyway).

So the inspiration for the following collection of essays has been taken from those materials of Levenson's I've studied, as well as his students Hale Dwoskin and Larry Crane, plus others. I mention the specific books and recordings as I go. This series of essays which follow are just my effort to simplify Levenson for our age – and to apply what he said could be improved in his own teachings, so that you can get the Freedom, Happiness, and Joy for yourself, that have always been there, patiently waiting...

- - - -

Now, this note: originally these essays were all posted individually on a blog. So while they are each true to their own point – and each was only included due to the points they cover – in various ways, the may cross and re-cross some of the same specifics.

Consider these as flowers on the same tree – however similar, no two are identical. Each contributes to the beauty of the whole.

Feel free to skip around as you want, although I've worked to organize them in related sections and produce a linear flow of thought you can follow as you see fit. Consider each section to be another branch of the same tree.

The point is, as all the authors before this point cover different aspects of the same principles, use these essays as well to develop your own system or philosophy that will help you find that "path up the mountain." Treat them as a buffet table of ideas and pick those which make the most sense (and are the most filling) for you personally.

And as the Irish say, "May your road rise up to meet you."

The Way: How to Begin - as Freedom Takes Over Your Life

When searching for Freedom becomes more important to you than seeking the World and all it's "benefits", then this search tends to "take over" your life.

Of course, that's a good thing. Because all your own innate Freedom starts rushing to the surface of your consciousness and everything starts to align with it. Of course, as you go, you have to keep releasing the bliss that shows up.

These notes are coming straight from the heart, so please study them carefully. They may seem disjointed, or non-sequitur. But they are simply notes. I'm working to get these out and to you as fast as I can so that you get the main points which have to be told.

Let's have some basics here:

Negatives tend to disappear and get replaced by "less-positives". Because negatives don't exist – every time you say a don't, a can't, a won't – anything with a not in it, it's a lie. The universe only exists on positives and less-positives. The positive always exists, even in very low levels. The terms "negative" and "not" and others like that, are just placeholders. They tell you to consider the idea that there is so little of something that it might not be perceptible. Nothing, for all practical purposes. But there is always still something there.

It's like that analogy Haanel uses – you don't go into a dark room and start shoveling out the dark – you turn on a light. Dark isn't the opposite of light – it's a varying condition of the *lack* of light.

And so you can see the uselessness of a concept such as Hell or Damnation. Practically, there are interpretations of the Bible which say the worst place possible is just the worst you can imagine. (Some literal translations of the Gospels say that Hell was actually a garbage pit – which is probably the worse spot on earth for most of us.) Not that any Hell, Hades, or other Damnation actually exists – except in your mind. Practically, as Heaven is within you, so is Hell. Your choice. (Of course, this is just my idea – reject it if it doesn't forward truth for you.)

Now, a point of disclaimer:

These ideas are mostly directly inspired by Levenson's book, "Keys to the Ultimate Freedom", but also from his tapes as noted. Other sources are listed (and see the Resources section at the end). If something I say doesn't make sense, just reject it and move on. If you need it later, it will be there for your use. The reason for these two statements is simple – it's your own Freedom, Happiness, and Joy which are important, not mine or anyone else. For all you know, I've ceased to exist on this earth for a very long time by the time you read this. Dust doesn't care. History doesn't care. Death doesn't care. Legacies are built to serve those who haven't attained their own Freedom. So I'll be pointing out things – more as a tour guide than anything else. If someone said something important, I'll work to get it exactly and post it as a quote. If you want to look it up, then do so. (If I mention something that isn't on the Internet broadly, I'll reference that source so you can find it. But realize that it's not the messenger that is important, it's the message.)

The key point is that you find your own Freedom. No one can do it for you. You can't buy it in any store. No one can give it to you. You have to earn it. And this earning is by doing less and less and less. Hard work isn't part of it. Dedication is.

We'll be going down that road of having a "burning desire". Like tying a carrot (or the best treat you can imagine) to a long pole that you stick out in front of you - just out of reach. Of course, you keep moving forward to try to get that treat.

Freedom is like those sirens the sailors used to hear, but the sirens don't call you to sail into their rocks, they call you to quit spending your time sailing around chasing after treasures and instead start living in earnest.

Freedom Is (period.) - 68

As Freedom calls you, a lot of stuff is going to drop away as less important and less vital. Just let it go.

How to Get Everything You Really Want Out of Life - Easier Than You Thought...

The trick is that everything you really want is already present...

Of course, my view on this - and how I write about it - has gone through several incarnations, and may still change. But I think I've finally gotten down to a basic line of application and theory which has undercut everything I've studied up to this point.

And I reserve the right to revise this without notice.

One of my first attempts at this came from a book I compiled, called "Mystic Marketing" – which does work where applied. Essentially, it has you hone your ability to concentrate on what you want and deliver this to the Universe to manifest.

If you're familiar with "The Secret", you'll recognize that many teachers recognize the first statement above is true. And to get anything else to show up around you, there just has to be a change in your considerations.

Of course, Levenson's releasing technique releasing technique is the prime way to accomplish changing your thoughts and calming the mind. Just acknowledge and accept what's there and let it go. Follow that by reviewing what it is that you want and release on both having to have it and not having it. As well as being separate from it, or having to be one with it.

Sure, that's all a mouthful. You could also just simply have it show up by just releasing all the time. Whatever "it" is.

But all the classics, Wallace Wattles, Charles Haanel, Napoleon Hill – even the real "old" authors such as Genevieve Behrend and her mentor Thomas Troward. All of these just point out that whatever you really want is already there – the Universe is in a constant state of delivering exactly what you've asked for. And old writings two and three centuries earlier – and even to points before written history – all of these say this same point. You already really possess anything you are looking for.

In fact, they all also say or support the fact that this Universe is only thought-created – and that all the life-mechanics we go through simply justify the thought. All the "scientific" studies are just ways to rationalize the miracles-as-usual which surround us. And all this scientific explanation machinery is foundering on quantum physics – where they found out that what you think predisposes the outcome of the experiment...

Our modern approach to this is to recognize that we perhaps haven't asked for exactly what we want, but have asked for something else. "The Secret" has several teachers saying to rephrase anything with a negative in it – which has long been known to NLP practitioners, but is actually an ancient datum: the mind doesn't recognize a negative. So when you say you don't want something in your life, it shows up in spades.

Don't = do not = do.

Don't want = do want.

Of course, our thoughts are often jumbled, because of the non-optimal mental habits we've been keeping. We've built up all these survival patterns of thinking to keep us secure and survive. And the Levenson releasing technique allows us to release ourselves from the effects of these perpetual thought circles which have been keeping us suppressed, un-free, unhappy, stressed-out, miserable.

And as you release more and more, the mind quiets. You aren't filling it with endless thinking any more. *Then* you can figure out what you *really* want out of life – and it begins to show up.

Until then, it's much like walking around the living room with the lights turned off. You know roughly where the furniture is, but not exactly – and your shins take a beating until you finally find the light switch.

Now, the ability to concentrate on what you want isn't actually something taught in our government schools. And to a great extent, we train ourselves out of this by watching TV and popular movies. We tend to deaden our mind, to turn control of it over to others. Which is why advertising found on these "boob tubes" are so inane and stupid. Psychologists Maslow and Cialdini worked this over quite well that our motivations are what we've been trained by our culture to accept.

This just brings my continuing advice to the fore – that you have to turn off the TV, radio, and put aside the national newspapers in order to start improving your life. (The Internet is OK, providing you use it in strict moderation.) All of the above just keep your mind excited and reinforce the bad mental habits you've been carrying around with you all this time.

You are going to have to release these mental habits before you can make any real progress in getting what you really want.

The Great Releasing Technique Experiment - Freedom with no cost

This is no experiment, this is life at its fullest.

While this may seem adventurous to some, it is really every persons' adventure. Because if you are reading this, you are seeking peace, personal freedom, happiness, joy, prosperity – whatever you want to call it and in all its incarnations.

But I'm not here to simply parrot or explain Levenson, Dwoskin, Crane, Seretan, or anyone else. These are just my own approach to this particular subject of personal clearing – if you want to call it that.

The Rules:

1. Cut out all TV, radio, newspapers, magazines other than what you need to directly live your life. Sure, if we could create a cave with temperature control and sufficient food to live indefinitely, then you could cut everything out – all contact with the world for the period you are working at this. But realistically, no.

My own compromise is to live on a farm and by choice with little contact with people other than a very few close family and whoever I have to deal with to get the farm business done. My freelance is on the web, so I work at this. And try to keep from going down rabbit holes by staying focused with exact actions to do daily.

The idea is to calm the mind and not let disturbances set it off again.

2. Understand the various release techniques fully. Get the books, listen to as many tapes as you have to. Get all this homework done as you can. Keep these to hand as reference, but don't refer to them constantly. Get the basics down to simplicities that you can easily apply.

3. Release constantly. Everything that comes up – until nothing comes up at all. Find your intuitive Self – and work out how to release that as well. Release all bliss as well. You'll know when you're done. Release stuckness when you get stuck, if you do.

4. Take no examples of anyone else as standards or goals for yourself. Not Lester, not the Christ, not anyone. In fact, release all goals and all personal standards of behavior you had earlier set. Become completely hootless about anything and everything. Attain or acquire anything and everything you need by releasing.

5. When you run out of things to release, and the world is perfect all the time, answer: "What Am I?"

- - - -

That's the sum of it.

Doesn't mean you don't do anything, but it does mean you have to release constantly. Listening to TV or radio or any "news" just sets you back, as these are just distractions and arbitrarily give you more to release. You have to want your own freedom more than you want the world. It doesn't mean you can't have amusements – but these have their own costs in time. How fast you re-acquire your personal Freedom depend on how much time you devote to it.

What we are working at is to get as high as we can, as fast as we can – and that upper energy level will allow much faster releasing of broader concepts.

The key points are to get the world off your back until you are fully released. I'm not going to say you are going to become a Master – that is between you and your Self. I don't say you are going to do or achieve anything. If you follow these steps at all, what you get out is what you put in.

- Get the world off your back,

- Know and understand the basics so you can apply them simply.

- Release constantly.

- And when you run out of things to release and the world is perfect all the time, answer the question: "What Am I?"

I'm not saying this is easy or hard to do. Your mileage may vary.

It is just the approach I'm taking.

How you Release - Simply, Easily, Effectively.

Here's a disclaimer right off the bat: All I know is what I know. I haven't attended any seminars or special training in the Levenson releasing techniques. And I give great credit to Larry Crane, Hale Dwoskin, Stephen Seretan, and others for forwarding this subject and making more workable.

All I say here is what I've learned for myself.

My own training was being given a bootleg CD (a few, actually) and being impressed with this material. And then I went out on the Internet and found everything I could about Lester Levenson and his releasing technique. Through this, I found digital copies of out of print books, and other recordings of various quality.

But the truth of this as a very direct subject shone through.

There are two steps to the Levenson releasing technique:

1. Accept what is.

2. Let it go.

And it's no more complicated than that.

I and others occasionally have problems with letting something go, and in many cases it's just being stuck – so you let go of the stuckness.

Other than that, I don't see a big problem with anyone applying it to any and every area of their life. It does nothing but improve things.

Sure, I've been studying self-help books for years and was some 20+ years in Scientology and before that had spent several years in Bible Study as well as being an agnostic and all sorts of other studies as well as a few post-graduate degrees. Now, after 50-some years on this planet, the Levenson releasing technique comes my way and explains what I've been rejecting out of all these other studies – and actually made them all start working again.

But don't think I am going to tell you how this is any sort of abundance course, or how you can make be making money working from home, or use the law of attraction to create all sorts of prosperity, health, and incredibly loving relationships – because that's simply not where I'm at on this. Sure, releasing will help you with your business, with your love-life, with the abundance of wealth, with your quality of health – and help you get it all effortlessly – but: so what?

Once you get everything you want in your life, what then?

You see, what works for you is just that – it's what works for you. There are many paths up the mountain (as I often say) but no two are identical. Each and everyone of us have to make their own path, or find it. And that path isn't the same as the one the person on either side of you is using.

For me, Levenson's releasing technique is a key point to use in combination with other material in order to make my own progress toward personal Freedom – or Enlightenment (since Freedom is already within us – so is Enlightenment, actually...)

And this is why I also write about this stuff at length. Because I consider a few things to be vital truths - at least for me:

1. I am only here to help others.

2. Whatever I want to attain or have is best attained or acquired by helping others attain or get whatever it is that they want.

3. Finally, that the whole universe runs on these two statements above. Period.

Now you can and should disagree with me on any or all of the above. Because it's not true until it's true for you.

But I've had incredible gains after learning (teaching myself) the Levenson releasing technique. And so I recommend it to others – as many as will listen to what I have to say.

Since I hadn't ever told you how easy it is to release, I thought to tell you.

Cheers! – and Good Hunting!

The 7 Simple Steps to Releasing for Personal Development

(Excerpted and extracted from the tape series "The Way" these notes describe a very direct manner of re-achieving your personal Freedom. And whether you're looking for life's abundance or how to get rich – it's all in these 7 simple steps of Levenson releasing technique...)

The steps:

1. *Want Freedom more than you want the World.*

2. *Take all your joy from within by releasing.*

3. Make the decision to go Free and then do it.

4. Go directly to the fear of dying and then release it.

5. Get everything from here on by direct releasing.

6. Be not the doer. Be the witness. Let go and let God.

7. Make your behavior that which a Master would do.

Once you decide to get moving on the path to total freedom, you will eventually make it out. The only reason these materials exist is to enable you to do it in a single lifetime, this one.

All the joy there is in life already exists within you. You just have to release all the limitations that you hold in place to keep this from showing up.

You set up the decision to go Free and just work at it. Don't resist anything, just push this right on up and you'll make it. Keep striving for this and you'll arrive. The more you concentrate on it, the faster it shows up.

All the other points – control, approval, security are all based on the fear of dying. Simply go to the central fear of dying – release it directly and completely – and the rest falls away. You have to quit trying to make the body survive – to exist through the body. (But it's suggested by several releasing technique counselors that you spend significant time releasing before you try this on your own – it has at times made people physically sick.)

There's nothing you want that can't be more easily and rapidly acquired (it will show up faster) if you just release on the fact of it's being there now. Look for anything that comes up when you accept the goal of that product or service being present right now in your life.

Don't effort at doing anything. Flow with the actions around you. You'll get intuitive insight on what actions you should be doing. Just be the witness to what is going on. You'll see the actions happening around you and you only just have to move with what you should do to achieve harmony in your own life and the world around you. Just let go of any effort and let the God in you do the doing that makes sense in the moment.

Act only in ways as a Master would. The more you just follow the Master presence which is already within you, the more will show up on the external "you" which everyone else then sees. You will then start intuitively to do the right actions, the necessary actions, the harmonious actions. And all things that you actually want in life will show up for you. What you want will change. What you want now isn't necessarily what you are going to wind up with – it will be a lot better, a lot bigger, far more of it than you want or think you want right now. Just get off the thinking and act only as a Master would. And let it show up around you.

- - - -

Whether you use Hale Dwoskin's techniques, or those of Larry Crane, or someone else – it doesn't matter. The point is that you find a method you can use on a continual basis. As you simply incorporate this into your daily mental habits, life becomes more direct and easier. Try it and see – don't just accept what I say. It won't be true until you've tested it for yourself.

Be the Author of Your Own Life Story. Truth and Responsibility

It's just too easy to say life is an open book. Especially when you say that someone else wrote it. But practically, there is no way around the fact that you are the author of your own life's story – the plot is yours alone, as well as the actions of practically all the characters in it.

I've been known to remark - often - about how the Golden Rule works around you all the time, that it can't be avoided or negated – it just is. Regardless of whether you "believe in it" or not, regardless of your faith. It just is.

Golden Rule

So that means, essentially, that regardless of your relationship with God, a great deal of what is around you right now is the result of your actions or inactions – if not all of them.

Now this takes you a bit beyond "The Secret" and what it said. Wallace Wattles (Science of Getting Rich) and others have made a great deal about your needing to be grateful for what you have in order to get more of anything you want. And that is all very true. But this concept above takes you a bit beyond that point.

It really takes you a step toward what Lester Levenson is talking about with his original releasing technique teachings. And this is where the common sense of "The Secret" meets the extreme metaphysics of Levenson.

The world around you, for all practical purposes (and within believable limits) is what you put there. If you've been critical toward others, you've gotten some criticism into your life in return. Where you've been caring and appreciative, you've seen some care and appreciation come into your life. Where you have open-handedly helped others achieve their own goals – you've received some unexpected help with whatever you have elected to achieve.

So with this we are seeing that the more responsible you are for the world around you, the more it turns closer to Heaven on earth. Because the Kingdom of Heaven is within you, as Jesus said. You just have to "let your light shine" so that it starts showing around you.

And that's where Levenson's release technique comes into play.

What is holding you back from simply being gracious with everyone around you and helping everyone in sight to be and do their best for the people who surround them? Our own thoughts are traitors, as Shakespeare said. That is exactly the problem we face – the prison for our soul is composed of those habitual thoughts we've kept to tell us how to react in various circumstances. Fear, anger, distrust, apathy, worry, anxiety –

all these reactions are those we've put there and still hold in place.

Get rid of these and you can see and foster more good in people around you. And more and more of that goodness then comes into your own life. Because the Golden Rule is inexorable. Happens anyway. Like it or not.

Releasing just allows you to get over all those negative thoughts, releasing allows your own internal happiness and joy to show up more and more frequently. No effort.

The next time you feel like doing something to someone that you wouldn't like having happen to you – try this:

- Pause for a moment.

- Take a deep breath in through your nose and out through your mouth – slowly. Take several if you want.

- Then just accept that emotion which is coming in. Let it really show up in full – don't act on it, just let it be.

- Then see if you can simply let it go, release it.

- Now, go ahead and treat that person the way you'd like it.

Too often, it will easily ddrop away on just those few steps. (Hale Dwoskin, Stephen Seretan, and Larry Crane have more steps you can learn for free on how to do this over at their respective Levenson releasing technique sites.)

But as you keep this up, and constantly work to help others around you in just the way you'd like to have happen to you if you were in their situation – keep releasing all feelings you have coming into you which tell you not to act that way... Then the world around you starts to even out. And you'll see gratitude start swelling up in you for everything around you – because you are being responsible for that world and are appreciative of all that you helped bring into your life.

Try it and see for yourself.

Section II - What This Can Mean for You

The Less Important Live Among Us as The Greatest.

It's obvious that Masters walk this earth. And they don't particularly care a hoot about being "discovered" or "exposed". Because they really don't give a hoot about anything. They do their job easily, effortlessly, and live their life in comfort. Mostly unknown, they don't seek the spotlight necessarily – since that is a trade-off and can get in a person's way in living life.

The key thing is to let your own Freedom shine out from within. You don't hide a light under a basket, you let it shine.

The usual disclaimer: My ideas on this are just that – discount them immediately and make them your own or reject them.

 There are some old phrases from the releasing technique which I'll repeat here. "Be not the Doer, Be the Witness." "Let go and Let the Universe."

You have to get your Self out of the way so you can let the Universe within you shine through. You already have all the answers to any problem or situation right within you. All you have to do is let it out. There is no effort in it. Just let go and let the Universe. Let the Universe what? Anything it damned well pleases.

That's the point. The You gets in the way. There is a way of intuitional living you can adopt (or not – your choice). What this does is connect you with a fountain-well of constant inspirational and motivational. All answers are there, all solutions are there. It's the Universe just wanting to peek out behind that "solid" facade called Self.

The idea here is that it's much easier to go through life by letting the Universe guide you.

Your life could be that of a Master – calm, quiet, perfect in every way. Just try what is covered in this book for yourself.

Speed up and Get There Faster Without Moving at All.

This isn't some sort of Alice in Wonderland scene where you have to run as fast as you can just to stay in the same place. (Although many of us may have had jobs which were like that at times.)

The Levenson phrase is "Don't release to get high. Go high to release."

As you reach higher levels by releasing, learning more and more to seek more freedom at every turn instead of more world, as you learn to quit doing and witness more – you reach a very high internal energy level where things will just start disappearing on their own.

The release technique is too simple. A lot of people have worked to make it reachable by others – since if it were complicated, everyone would know it. But when you grasp the basics, then it can and should become second nature.

The whole point is to get the habit of releasing to replace the bulk of the mental habits you have. If you have any emotion coming in, then release it. If you aren't at peace constantly, release whatever it is that you have your attention on (or are trying to keep from having your attention on.) You want to find your own internal peace (which actually comes from the Universe) and let it flow out from you into the world you live in. Anything that blocks this flow – just let it go.

You want to get to these high levels as fast as you can, since this will make that flow a torrent. Of course, any bliss that shows up, release that as well. It's not a state of ecstasy you want to achieve. It's a calm, almost serene and simple way of living where there is no rush, there is no excitement, everything is just fine, everything is just perfect.

And it's that way all the time.

So get releasing down to just a two-step process – you see something, then you let it go. Eventually, things just start cascading, as your internal flow just rolls things out of your system faster than you can even consider what it was that you had your attention on a few moments ago – but that's OK, it doesn't matter: the Universe is perfect.

Probably won't happen overnight. But you may wind up woken up in the night with some inspiration, something you have to do right now. As you let go and let the Universe, this will happen more and more. But it's always for the better – you're just going to get rid of some old "hold-me-back" habit and replace it with something better – or nothing at all.

Yes, this changes your life radically. As you are able to let these old things go, then your life will improve to that degree. The stuff you hold onto is holding you back. While we can't all necessarily just move off into remote caves or monasteries to live lives of quiet contemplation, most of us won't be called to do that. Just not the way this Universe operates – at this level, anyway.

The point is to be as responsible as you can for your own earlier mental habits and release these as fast as you can find them. Release being stuck if you find yourself stuck (just another mental habit). Release everything and get everything by releasing.

The World around you changes for the better – just to that exact degree you release.

The Unimportance of Importances

Nothing is really important.

Sure, there are things you should do to keep living on this planet. But let the Universe show you what these are.

Take "your passion in life". Most people draw a blank when you ask them what they feel their purpose in life is – what they are here to accomplish in this lifetime. But that's usual. Most people have the bulk of the Universe walled off so it can't get out. Most people "work" at "jobs" to "make money" or "make a living."

And some people get paid to play baseball or some other sport for a living. They retire when they are in their 30's or 40's and manage real estate or golf all day, or some such. And the bulk of us these days have several careers.

I know of an organization that set about to find out the basic purpose of all their employees. They set up a huge program and put all their staff through it. But when the results started coming out, they found out that a small percentage of people were simply quitting their jobs as it wasn't what they really wanted to do with their lives. Of course that was a disruption. So management quickly came down with a correction that revised the program into "finding what their purpose for their job was". This apparently stopped the turnover. But it was trying to put a cork in the genie's bottle. (Frankly, they already had turnover all the time because people were frustrated from their denied purposes already. So their revision solved nothing in fact.)

I was one of those people who saw this and simply moved out of their way – into the Way which the Universe was going. Like was said earlier – you have to let your light shine. It's far easier and more comfortable than any corporate job working for someone else – unless that is exactly what you should be doing.

The Levenson releasing technique just helps you find and confirm your passion.

If you're happy, contented, and everything is going fine around you – then you are on the right path for you.

Because the world is perfect.

And this is why I don't mention earlier Masters here, or quote the legacy or writings of others. What good would it do? Someone pulling off a miracle just builds resistance in others so they can't follow as easily. Sure, if everyone were pulling off miracles every day, then it's common place. Like flying in an airplane, or driving along a road while you're sitting still inside a car. Or holding a piece of plastic to your ear and talking to someone on another continent. Miracles in the 1800's – not today.

Learn from the world around you, but more importantly, let the Universe already within you give you the lessons you need next. Let your light shine.

Here is one importance you can and should reject until you possibly can make it your own – testing it for yourself:

Whatever you want, give it away to someone else first in order to make it show up. That's one version of the Golden Rule. Treat others as you would want to be treated. Cheer someone else up in order to be happiest yourself. Help others be successful and your success is assured. If you don't have something, figure out how to help someone else get it – first.

Of course that flies in the face of any idea of competition. But competition is a lie, anyway, isn't it? "Level playing fields" are fantasies. No such thing. Winners simply out-create others. Sports are putting a bunch of talented people onto a arena where they are hampered by various rules and "now-your-supposed-to's" so they can excel to produce a very, very narrow range of accomplishments. The Universe isn't like that. Everyone excels in their own specialty. And there are just as many specialties as their are people.

So this of course comes in as: "many paths up the mountain". What is important for you isn't as important for the next guy.

Listen to the Universe within you – your own particular flavor. That's where your Freedom is going to shine from. And it's *your* Freedom, not the next guy's.

Get Everything You Want by Giving Everything Away

Here's some Levenson quotes:

> *"Let go of all your attachments and you'll be so light, it will be hard to stay on the ground."*

> *"Let go of all your desires and you reach the ultimate level of happiness. And when you put a thought out, it shows up."*

> *"Let go of all desires, all attachments and all these other things – and be free."*

> *"The more you let go of attachments, the happier you get – and the easier it is to get things."*

> *"We started out playing a game and wound up thinking happiness was outside of ourselves."*

Do you see how this works? Of course, the usual disclaimer: reject all of this unless and until you can make it your own, deciding and proving for yourself that it has use or applicability in your own life. That you can maybe get something out of it.

Now, the world is full of ego-traps. And the physical things you see around you are just the symbols of these. Money, houses, clothes, cars, planes, video games – all these things aren't real. Most of them would disappear in a fire or other catastrophe.

But a person who knows how to get them can replace them at any time.

A person who is dependent on them is devastated when they lose them – and even when they think of losing them. This person often doesn't have them and is just stuck in the desire for them. But even if they get what they want, they can't keep it.

Because they don't simply see them as symbols for other ideas. Money is a humankind thing. Doesn't exist naturally. You can't eat it, but you can use it to get others to give you food. Won't buy love, but you can get someone to have sex with you, or even marry and live with you for the rest of your life. Can't make you happy, but it can get stuff which will distract you from your unhappiness for a little while.

So the stuff around you isn't the real you. That real you is only what you find out it is. You have to start letting the Universe within you shine out.

Start the habit of releasing all the time – any feeling or thought about anything – just let it go. Use the release technique constantly. Then you can easily get anything and everything that you need or want. Precisely because you get off the artificial needs and invented wants.

Make releasing so regular in your life that you don't think about it, it's just second nature.

And quit efforting to get, or acquire, or achieve, or attain anything. Everything you really need/want will come to you if you just let the Universe within and around you bring it to you.

All this effort people put into getting stuff, that's just making it harder. That's a real game. Level playing field and all that nonsense. If you want to really win the game, quit playing it. Just let the game play itself. Be the witness up in the stands.

How to Make Your Own Luck

Being "lucky" is something no one has really ever been able to define. Mostly because the don't know how it happens or how to create it.

Some people "feel" lucky and won't buy a lottery ticket unless they have that feeling. But they can't tell anyone else how to feel that way. It runs in some families, particularly among females, but again – there's no particular DNA strand or link or coding that really says what makes lucky people that way. (And if they did, I suppose they think we're going to have some sort of re-coding surgery to "correct" it? Painful.)

What I've known about luck up to this point (and before I tell you about a recent breakthrough) – was two things:

> *1. You can only "make" your own luck – by positive thinking and pro-active living.*

> *2. The old quote, "Luck is opportunity met with preparation."*

And while you can see that these are related, and both quite sensible, they still fall quite short.

- While you can be as pro-active as you want, this means luck is dependent on working hard – and you can work yourself to death thinking as positive as you want and still have horrible luck – even "dying in the traces."

- If you don't know how to prepare for the luck which is supposed to fall into your lap, you might as well stay in school for the rest of your life – because how are you supposed to know what luck to prepare for?

The way I've stumbled on lately seems the most direct route.

I use Levenson's releasing technique.

Of course, this is "Law of Attraction" on steroids. You simply see what you really want out of life and release all the reasons you can't have it, or aren't worthy, or how having it "gets back at" people, or whatever feeling that comes in when you get that concept. You don't push the other feelings away, you just let them go.

Of course, Larry Crane and Hale Dwoskin have their own ways and approaches to get this done. But they are both based on the original Lester Levenson research.

And this really boils down to just getting the effort out of your life – which is really just improving your "luck-ability" score. Anyone you've ever heard about or met wasn't working hard or studying their butts off when that lucky event showed up in their life. They were taking it easy and the luck wasn't even expected.

That's what releasing does. You get all the effort out of your life, and definitely, certainly quit thinking about it.

effortless living

In earlier posts, I've covered this as "intuitional living" – and now we could actually call it effortless living.

When the person who is luckiest in life firt considers something, they release every thought or feeling they have about it and then lets the Universe bring it to them on it's terms. Like Wallace Wattles said about using the normal lines of industry and commerce.

Sure, there's a few other details to it, like always picturing it in the Now – so you always see yourself as having this already in your life – but it's really simple and easy once you study the basics.

So I invite you to check out the the authors' sites above and put these into your life as continuing habits.

And get incredibly lucky all the time at everything.

The Universe is One Big Joke - and We are the Punchline, not the Butt of it.

The Universe can be seen to be one huge joke. And the people still here never got the punchline. Far from being the butt of the joke, they actually started the joke themselves.

For the Universe is built out of limits. We agreed to have limits and so we have them.

I do a lot of volunteer work for an outdoor education center called Scattering Fork. We take small groups out in the woods on what is called a low-ropes course, and have them do team challenges – which make them think and act outside any particular box they are in. I've started telling them that there are 1) the rules for that particular challenge, 2) the safety rules for that challenge, and 3) anything else they want to make up for themselves. The first two sets you have to follow – but you can do whatever you want with the third set.

And it takes awhile before they figure out that they set far more limits than the challenge requires.

That is really a microcosm of this Universe we are in. None of this that surrounds you is serious. Start releasing all the time, consistently, and you'll see this to be true. You'll find yourself calmly cheerful, optimistically expectant for the next thing that the Universe is bringing you.

People who are serious about the world around them haven't figured out what the joke is. And might not for a very long time.

But those who have will just smile quietly and ask you if you need any help with that...

Because that is actually how easy it all is. This world around us is a piece of cake, a cake-walk.

It's not serious, it's a joke. Be the punchline.

How I Get Rid of Nagging Worries and Stress

The trick to eliminating worry, anxiety and stress is actually easier than it looks.

But it's taken me some months of practice on top of years of study in order to figure it out. And I didn't need any expensive life coaching to help me.

The simplicity is using the Levenson releasing technique to get rid of those continuing thoughts that seem to rattle around your mind and distract you so much.

You just follow these direct steps:

Releasing
★!

> 1. *Accept that nagging thought – let it be. Don't resist or fight it any more.*

> 2. *Then simply be willing to let it go and then just let it go.*

Sure, Larry Crane and Hale Dwoskin have more steps you can use to do this – and you should check them out if you're interested.

But keep it as direct and uncomplicated as possible.

★!!

The only refinement I have to contribute is that you don't want to be figuring out why or "how come" or "what it all means". You just want to get to the point that you can accept the thought for what it is and then let it go. Dwoskin was telling me that through his tapes months ago, but until I actually got down to the simplicity of it, I was still looking for symbolic or metaphysical reasons – or considering that something was happening somewhere that I was connected to.

Sure, there might be reasons or explanations or connections to others. But you won't hear about those through thinking about it. In "Go Thunk Yourself, S'more!" I came upon the idea of "Intuitive Analysis" – where you just let your intuition start answering the questions you come up with. It's a much faster and easier way of studying things than most people use. And your intuition, like any muscle or skill you use, gets better and stronger with practice.

Your thinking speeds up incredibly. And your stress drops away remarkably.

But if your thinking is filled with negative, critical, stressful, worrisome, or other useless thoughts – then it's not all that comfortable. The trick is to get rid of those type of thoughts and start appreciating the intuitive and inspirational glimpses you have – and these are always accompanied by happiness, joy, acceptance, courage, and peace.

This is "being in the zone", or better – living in the zone.

You have to get the contra-survival thoughts out of your system. Look at them for what they are and then let them go. Don't think more thoughts about them, just let them go.

If it's peaceful, accepting, courageous – then you aren't really having your best thoughts. And those other thoughts just need to be let go. Like you are constantly working to help everyone around you, even those who have really "ticked you off" at some time in the past. Anyone you are working against, trying to control, or inhibit their success in some way – all this simply works against you. Golden Rule again. You are really just helping everyone around you to become more perfect – or to let their native perfection shine more brightly through.

Just get over those thoughts. Accept them as existing and then let them go. Too easy.

It works for everything. Every time you get some stress on your lines, if you practice just letting stuff go, then it gets easier and easier to live an incredibly peaceful and calm life. Everything goes well for you.

Too easy. And that's why people don't do it. They want something complicated and difficult.

But you can use this today and start getting all worry, stress, and negative emotions right out of your personal life. Right now. Try it and see. And start welcoming your native abundance and prosperity into your life as this "stress management" takes root.

And check out those other authors if you want to know more about how to apply it in your own life.

Section III – The World is Just as You Create It

All God's Children are Kahunas...

You know, we are all Masters in our own right. True. Just look inside and you see the perfection that you already are.

The ancient Polynesians had this completely right. Nowadays, when you say Kahuna, you either think of some surfer dude who always beats everyone else out in the competitions – or some mystic healer who can fire-walk, control nature, and maybe raise the dead.

But "Kahuna" always met something like "keeper of the secret", although that is a very loose translation (suitable for us ha-ole's who don't speak a word of it). There were kahuna's for every trade and business and activity. Our use would be "mentor" – as you would seek out these experts if you wanted to learn that skill or art. (Fishing kahuna's, weaving kahuna's, gardening/farming kahuna's, etc.)

And so, originally, there were kahunas all over the place. (Check out Wikipedia for these terms.)

It is even so today. Masters (kahunas/mentors) of any trade actually abound. Our approach with the Levenson releasing technique, is to enable everyone to master themselves as well.

My approach, different from most, is to tell you that you don't have to have a lot of money, or sexual partners, or servants, or impeccable health to be a complete success. You don't have to control vast estates of property and hundreds or thousands of employees to be a success.

But certainly, you need to be free of having to have approval from anyone else about what makes your success.

For the only person who can weigh in on your level of success is you. You either are doing what you want to do in life, or you aren't. And the only one who sets the decisions about what you should and shouldn't be doing is you.

That is the freedom which Levenson releasing technique brings – to be able to be, do, and have anything you want. You don't have to have money or prowess in order to accomplish whatever it is you want today.

If you want to stay at home and home-school the kids while maintaining the household, then that's perfectly fine. So is flying airplanes for a living. Anything you want to do that isn't hurting anyone else or illegal because of that fact – you should be able to simply learn to do as an expert in that field. A Kahuna. A Master.

And any Master of their craft does it with an ease that makes it seem like they were born to do just that. And it's probably true. For when a person is following their passion, it's something that they meant to do since they were born (or thereabouts.) But that doesn't mean you can only have one passion. Many people have several and either master all of them, or shift from one to another, mastering each in turn.

The key point in that is that they do it with ease. That is where Levenson releasing technique comes in. Masters release on everything and anything which interrupts or interferes with their practice of their craft. And they live rather calm, peaceful lives. Even if it's a hut on the beach they have to rebuild every few years. Or if its a stone hut in the glens of Scotland so old that there's no record of when it was first built. Or the business executive who has been rising through the ranks for 20-30 years and stands a chance of being the COO or CEO soon. Or the administrative assistant who has seen those CEO's come and go – but knows how to help them all be a success through her mastery of corporate policy and human behavior.

There are Masters who walk this earth and they need not be famous or wealthy or outrageously lucky.

And the reverse is true. People who win lotteries are often bankrupt and further in debt a couple years later – because they never learned how to manage wealth. People who have rented their whole lives aren't necessarily ready for home ownership. Because a politician is able to get elected due to his great speeches doesn't mean he's ready to be a statesman.

As well, most people are hampered by popular success – celebrities often no longer have any life of their own once they've "made it." So being a quiet success and having everything you could want is just fine with most people.

My point here is that you are looking for personal freedom, above and beyond any fame or fortune. The society around you worships these ego-traps. That doesn't mean you have to.

You have to want freedom more than you want the world. And once you get yourself on that route, you'll walk it right on out. Sure, others may pass you by, or maybe you suddenly attain it in a flash after pursuing it for years and years.

And after you Master yourself, then what? Practically, the release technique has been used to help people become millionaires and resolve relationships, and create huge successes. But the people who only used it for those material things wound up in trouble again, sooner or later. Because money, fame, fortune – all these are part of the World. They are not part of Freedom.

Doesn't mean you'll be broke and lonely – those are also part of this world. When you look for the Freedom, Peace, and Joy which have always lay within you – just waiting to be let out – then the world gives you anything you want. Because you don't need it anymore.

So: become the Master you already are. Let your light shine.

Love and Life Without Limits

You may recall that we've gone over this point that all people, all humankind (and this also extends to all life and maybe even inanimate matter according to the quantum physicists) – that we are all connected some how, some way.

The only thing that keeps us separate is our own oddball ideas that we are separate.

And, of course, you eliminate these oddball thoughts by using the releasing technique constantly.

Once you do that, do you know what happens?

Unconditional love.

At that point, there is no one you can't get along with, no one that distresses you, no person or animal which doesn't respond positively when you communicate with it.

Because without all those thoughts holding you back, you are in a state of unconditional love with the world around you.

It's kind of weird, I guess, to think this way. (But you can always release that "weirdness" thought, can't you...)

Our most ancient philosophical and religious traditions hold this to be true. We are all connected.

Which gives another reason for quieting the mind. What you think, others can experience. You can't disconnect or shut down those lines. They are hard-wired, always on.

But you can quiet your mind, constantly release the thoughts that come in. You can live in peace and constant happiness – which is then what you are sending out to the world.

You can express unconditional love to those around you.

Now this doesn't mean you just lay down and become a victim – far from it. In fact, people who can't control their negative thoughts will start to stay away from you. Because they also know that the Golden Rule works regardless. And they don't want to share those negative thoughts with you, as they'll come right back to them.

Of course you can suggest they learn the Levenson releasing techniques. They may or may not take your suggestion. But just keep to your *own* level of internal peace and unconditional love and help them however you can.

Meanwhile, just continue to release any thought that comes in and work for that higher Goal of letting your own Personal Freedom come out.

The world around you will probably calm down immensely. Imagine a board room where all the executives in it were completely calm and in communication with each other. Makes for short meetings, very efficient.

So there is a reason for me to write this, for you to read it, for us to help people find their way to this technique.

See what you can do today to help someone else find their way to this. If it's a hassle, or a problem, then just sit and release on it.

And if you really want someone to find this, then take that as a Goal and release it as happening.

What We Are All After is Both Different and The Same

I'm not here to explain how the Levenson releasing technique works or to sell you on any particular kind or type. You'll find on this site many links to stuff about Levenson and all the teachers who have picked up his method and run with it.

You won't find a lot of Levenson or the others repeated much here. Reason being is that you need to find out for yourself. And the other point is that it really doesn't matter that much. When you understand the core material of how to release, then it's really simple after that. The hardest point is keeping going right on out.

This world we live in is filled with every reason not to continue and not to regain your Freedom. That Freedom, your own perpetual and personal peace and happiness – they all lie within as they always have. There are far too, too many stories where (like Conwell's "Acres of Diamonds") the person went off searching for something when he already had it right at home to begin with.

And all these teachers are taking the risk of all sorts of alienation and being compared to a scam and so on. Practically, they are just there to help you.

The way each of these various teachers help you is to educate you on the basics of releasing and then get out of your way to let you do it. They each have their systems, but it's no different in its basics.

All the problems, the pains, even the illnesses you have currently can be traced back to something you are holding on to for dear life. Problems are something you had in the past, and those solutions are being forwarded onto your current livingness. That is what all those collected thoughts are for – to simply prompt you with solutions.

However, the solution is the problem. And the only reason what you are facing still exists. Just face it, and let it go. That easy. That direct. Sure, you might have to get rid of an untold number of feelings and what-not thoughts which crop up just so you can then look at the basic scene – but the more you release, the easier it gets.

And that is why you need to develop the new habit of releasing constantly. Plus meanwhile, getting the TV, radio, newspapers, and anything else irritating out of your life. These just hold you back by giving you more to release.

You want to be releasing your basic feelings and thoughts – the ones which are holding you back all the time.

These basic negative-thought-habits can be worked backwards from a couple of ways:

> *Is your current thought or feeling the way you'd like to be treated?*
>
> *-or-*
>
> *Does this thought or feeling give me greater peace or happiness?*

If you answer no to either of the above, then just let it go. (But practically, as Hale points out, you want to release all thoughts anyway – since any thought or belief or consideration just holds you back. So release anything and everything that comes up.)

Then, once you get your mind quiet (at least enough so you can hear yourself think), then focus on something which would help you help others if it showed up in your life.

When that appears, get the idea of it showing up. And then release any negative feeling or thought that comes in. Like how it's impossible, or how people won't approve of you, or anything like that (as the taxes you are going to have to pay, for example). Just keep releasing about whatever it is that you'd like to show up until you can hold that idea of it showing up right in front of you easily.

Then simply let it go – and let the Universe figure out how to manifest.

And that's all you do on it. Period. Don't plan about it, don't think or worry about it. Just get the idea that it's completed and present - and then release it

Do that at least once a day. Some do it several times a day.

The rest of your day, you are working to help others – in any way you can. What makes the stuff you need and want show up faster is to help others with whatever it is that they are trying to get into their own lives. The more you help others, the faster your own life is filled with everything you need and want.

And that includes Personal Freedom.

Because the bottom line is that we aren't in this Universe to accumulate toys or other great stuff. You can only take the Love you feel within. So concentrate on going Free and helping others regain their personal Freedom.

The Trick is to Get the Ego to Undo the Ego, the Mind to Undo the Mind

As we've covered before, the mind and the ego are mostly composed of fiction. You've set up various thoughts as solutions to problems and hold them in place so you have a ready answer to anything that comes in front of you.

Unfortunately, these all have limits on your actual ability.

Thoughts are always, dependably, second to action. Action occurs without thinking. Like your blood circulating and your breathing. Sure, if you work at controlling your breathing, you can lower your heart rate.

To do this you have to concentrate.

To concentrate, you have to shut out other thoughts than the single one you are working on.

The problem is that most people can't do this. The vast majority of people just let those 50-60,000 thoughts a minute just race through their head, willy-nilly. And they try to get them to shut up by watching TV, listening to loud music, drinking alcohol, or taking other drugs – or some combination of the above.

If you want personal Freedom, you are going to have to quiet the mind.

Releasing technique allows you to just let go of the thoughts you've been holding onto and then the mind quiets. It's that simple.

And as you quiet the mind, your ego also tends to start to vanish. You start to look at the world for what it is, which needs very little thought. You can cease to be required to act, but just start watching this fantastic world around us go through its paces.

Sure, you are going to want to help out and do things – but you don't have to anymore. The difference is extraordinary.

You can now live your life exactly the way you've always wanted to – free from others' control, approval, or any need for security. You'll have few, if any, fears – including dying itself. When something does come up, you diredly look at it for what it is and then let it go.

Your ego just becomes a mirror of the world around you – like Teflon, nothing sticks to it. So you can simply start helping out wherever you are needed – or following the intuitive glimpses you receive to fulfill whatever passion you find you now have (which you've had all along, but were too busy thinking about it...)

There is no chance that you will lose your mind or your ego. You'll still be you. But you'll be more you, and your mind will be your own – not cluttered with others opinions of you or fears of what they might think or what might happen to you.

Try it and see.

Just be still for a moment – right now. Take whatever thought or feeling that comes in and accept it, then let it go. And then keep doing it. Funny enough, even if you think it's the same thought – it will be a lesser shadow of that thought, or a slightly different version. And as you keep confronting it and letting it go, it will get less and less.

Once you get releasing down to a consistent tool in your life, your mind will markedly quiet. You'll have more peace in your life, more happiness. You'll appreciate the world around you and have a lot more to give in return for all you've been given.

But you won't get there by just reading this.

Try it for yourself. See what results you can get.

Taking the Easy Way Out to Personal Freedom.

Part of this releasing idea is that you are taking the effort out of everything you do.

If all actions you took had no worries, no stress, no concerns, no negative feelings connected with them, how hard would they be to do?

How about having a day off, walking in the woods or along the beach with nothing bothering you, completely at peace? Easy, isn't it?

And when's the last time you were actually able to enjoy such an experience?

Which is why I suggest you get releasing as a constant mental activity instead of thinking.

Just being there in Nature is one of the most enlightening experiences a person can have. Yet most people are worried about where they parked their car, whether their sinuses are going to act up, if they turned off the stove at home, if they are missing a sports game, if that business deal on Monday will go OK...

They aren't just being there and enjoying the moment.

Releasing technique takes care of that.

So when you get all this releasing done, you are taking the effort of out all that you want to do. (Now notice that we are saying "want" and not "have" to do.) Even if someone asks you to help them with something, you can do it effortlessly if you aren't having some thought about how you don't want to be controlled or if they are going to approve of how you are doing it – and so on.

Effortless action.

You really wind up just being able to let go of all your "do-ership" Once you get the mind quiet, then the actions you should be taking just come to you. And almost do themselves.

Because you aren't concerned about anything and can simply stay detached and enjoy the peace of the action.

And you'll be filled with happiness. Actually, what is happening is that you are now radiating happiness. Then that helps everyone around you. Who doesn't like to be around a happy person?

But your happiness, your peace – are just waiting to be let out. You start to radiate your own happiness and peace when you quit wasting time on all those internal thoughts which have kept you "boiling over" all the time. You don't want to tell people what you are really thinking, as that isn't the way you'd like to be treated. So you hold it inside, along with everything else.

Where you are only at ease and in full communication with the world around you, then it's easy to just beam out happiness and your own internal peace. And you are a person that is in demand, as people love to share in your happiness and peace. But you really don't care whether or not other people like you – because the secret is in how much *you* love others, how much you can help others, how much you can give.

This open-handed help is the key. When you don't have to have anything, everything you really want or need will show up.

And then you can concentrate on simply going Free the rest of the way.

You'll know when you get there.

How to Take Control Over Everything that "Happens" to You.

Responsibility. That's the ticket.

One of the ways to speed up arriving at your Goal of personal freedom is to look over what has happened to you and check to see what it is that you did to cause that. Just hold that idea until the answer comes out of your subconscious (or any other part of your mind).

Then you'll have what you need to use the release technique.

Let's start at the bottom. You can release your feelings and they don't come back when you do. So you are responsible for all your feelings. After all, you recorded and put them there to begin with.

So when you have your feelings all sorted out – those random thoughts which come in and tell you how to feel about any given situation, as opposed to honestly reacting to the situation in front of you – then you can be responsible for creating those feelings which will best resolve that situation.

If you let your thoughts run your life, then you will always be a puppet on a string. Never responsible for what happens around you, never in control, always miserable.

When you take responsibility, you can take control, you can run your own life – be in charge, be confident of the outcome, achieve your goals.

Get into constant releasing, you can calm the mind and so see more clearly and take more responsibility and control in your life. As you do, your world becomes saner, better organized, simpler. Everything you need or want comes to you easier.

The next step after calming the mind and getting the world giving you everything and anything you want, is to answer, "What am I?" The answer to that is the capstone and you'll then have assumed complete responsibility and complete control over your world.

After that, it's up to you what you want to have, do, or be. But by then, you'll also have a really good idea of what those are.

But you won't get there by just reading my writings. You'll have to prove this for yourself. Otherwise, it's just more smoke and mirrors.

Check it out for yourself.

How Does Helping Others Help Me?

Helping others is the best way to speed up helping yourself. This is a very, very old idea – but it's almost disappeared in our modern "culture". (At least, until Levenson's releasing technique.)

The basic understanding below it is that we are all connected. The fallacy of our modern days, and how this game called the Universe became a "trap" was that the idea that we are all separate came around and got agreed upon.

If we aren't really connected, then it's OK to cause you harm, since it won't affect me, will it? But we had these reminders over and over and over, in every single major and minor philosophy and religious text: what you cause to others happens to you.

One of the most recent versions of this was "Treat others as you would like to be treated."

From this you can also see: "You have to give before you can get."

But it's all back to the point that we are all connected. Consider that old adage, "When you blame someone else, one finger is pointing at them, and three are pointing back at you." True, isn't it?

When you make someone feel bad, try to make them responsible for some situation or outcome, they feel bad, but you feel worse for having done that. Because it really just comes back to you, regardless of your considerations that you and that person aren't connected. Because you are – and down deep, you know it.

The Golden Rule works whether you believe it or not. It has nothing to do with beliefs, which are just thoughts, after all. It's the way this place was set up.

It's not just me saying it – but I tell you again: throw this away and check it for yourself. Watch others' lives and see if it doesn't happen to them like that. Go around cheering people up and see if you don't wind up more cheerful yourself. I don't advise anyone to go around being critical of others, but you probably look back at situations where you could have had a better outcome if you didn't criticize some person at that time.

Whatever you send out into the world comes back the same way. Some world-views hold that it comes back stronger (remember the three fingers above?) Others say it's an "eye-for-an-eye" type of phenomenon.

And so those people who are constantly deceiving people wind up being scammed themselves. And their money goes through their fingers like it wasn't theirs – which is true.

If you look over your life to see how you can improve the lives of others around you, and then take actions to improve those lives – you'll find that your own world improves to that same degree, or more.

So if you have a certain goal, help others achieve a similar goal they have – and then yours comes around that much faster.

And if you are after personal freedom, well...

Again – disregard what I say here and test it for yourself.

Section IV - Ultimate Freedom is Already Within You...

Not Just a Board Game: Live for Others in Order to Improve Your Own Life

There is really only one way to play the game of life. It's how you win.

Here's the bottom line – we are each individually and personally here to evolve, to get better, to make the best of life in this existence that we can.

Now, despite all the various "Laws" which have come up over the years, there is only one which is observed by every known religion, philosophic, and deep thinker on this planet – from time immemorial up to the present moment. Because it can be proved by every single person to exist and work.

"You only get back what you give away."

And this Law governs all success, all health, all the wants, dreams, and desires any human could expect to be, do, acquire, or attain in any life. It governs everything.

For some, this means "Love your neighbor as yourself." In other, older versions, "an eye for an eye, a tooth for a tooth."

(And there was that famous judge who put an end to the physical interpretation of this by agreeing that they could have their pound of flesh, but they could take only that – no blood or other fluids, nothing else.)

It is the Golden Rule in various versions, the Koran as well as the Bible, as well as ancient Druid texts, Hindu, Egyptian, and even earlier to the oldest philosophies that still survive in remote Polynesian islands.

We are all connected, there are no limits – so this rule says that when you hurt someone else, you hurt yourself, when you help someone else, you help yourself.

If you look at any millionaire, billionaire or better (or worse), you'll see that their money acquisition was on the backs of making other people rich at the same time. Ray Kroc (founder of McDonald's chain) made far more millionaires than he could count. Sam Walton's (Wal-Mart) expanded the sales of his suppliers many times over and was constantly working to improve the quality of life of his customers.

And that is the point to all this. To the degree you want to succeed in business, to get a great amount of income flowing toward you, to have a great home, nice stuff all around you – what do you have to do? What do you have to put your attention on?

The value of the product or service you are giving away.

Now, this doesn't mean we need to all be paupers. Quite the reverse. The oddest thing is that people won't value something, won't really use it, unless they have to give something of value in return. That is really the only reason profitable commerce continues to exist and communism/socialism always fails.

That Rolls Royce or that Cadillac is worth every penny. People will pay more for grass-fed beef which is raised naturally without hormones or excessive growth-producing chemicals – that they know where it came from. They'll pay several times what it took to create that beef and grow it for the two years it took to get to that size. Several times what they could have paid for that same beef at an auction yard and gotten it processed.

The added value is in bringing that specific product to them in a way they can use it best.

That's more to our point:

> *Any business or individual will only succeed to the exact degree that they help others succeed.*

For better or worse, Bill Gates' billions didn't arrive without giving a great deal of value to the computer industry and the personal computer buyers. Us, in other words. Take any industry leader and the also-rans. The best, the top of their class always, always gives value in greater quantity than they extract. Sure, there are "other factors" – but that is the key one. (And why Apple and the Linux community hold onto major shares of this market? Even better value.)

Your own success it really just this point:

> *Whatever it is that you want – help someone else get it, or better, several someone's. If you want help, help others. If you want to get rich, help others get rich. Want better health? – Work to improve others' health.*

There are examples all around of how this works.

The reverse is true – scam other people and you can't hold on to your own money. It's only temporary. If you want permanent wealth around you – you'll build wealth for others many times over in advance of your own, or at the same time. Not afterwards. (ripoff artists and politicians only have to hide when they are hiding something.)

This isn't a government job, which by definition is *always* taking something away by threat of force to "help" someone. I'll dissect government at another time. The deal here: all help is a personal thing. What ever you personally want, you have to help others get it first, or at least at the same time you do. Only then can you really fulfill your desires.

And once you get everything you could possibly want or need? Then just keep helping others learn how to do it for themselves. That's why all the really rich turn to helping others, even giving all their wealth away (like Buffet, Gates, and earlier, Carnegie, Rockefeller, etc.) Because now that you're there, what else do you have to do?

And how about those who amassed great fortunes only to die bankrupt — they didn't follow that Golden Rule. Help others all the time. Every way you can.

That's the only way out of this human existence we share on this planet at this time. Remember, Jesus said that "Heaven is within you." And hell-on-earth is just ignoring this one rule.

Your choice.

How You, Me, and the World Around Us Actually Works

You can get everything you want in life – and actually do. Whatever surrounds you is already what you've always wanted most.

So if you want something different, you simply have to change your mind.

But how to change it is the problem. Apparently, anyway.

Let's look at basics:

- You exist.
- You create the world around you by what and how you think.
- Your thoughts don't have to be on automatic all the time.
- You can change your feelings whenever you want.
- A thought about something in the future will never create anything – because the future never comes.
- Thinking about the past only changes your ideas about what happened before this point, if only a couple of micro-seconds ago. Those thoughts don't change the Now.
- Only creative thinking about what you want right Now will change what you are experiencing right Now.
- As everything you think comes back to you, thinking destructively about anyone or anything doesn't do or bring you any good.

There are a lot of therapies out there which cost a lot of money, but don't practically do anything (except make that person or organization rich) – because they deal with things that occurred in the past. What happened is done. Over. Kaput. Finished. Finis. You can't change it and thinking about it won't improve what is happening around you. Psychiatry, Scientology, any of these "sciences of the mind" which deal with regression – all these work ineffectively (and expensively) if at all. And they are always a continuing saga – you have to keep getting more sessions and paying more money from here on out.

The only reason we can't get what we want in life to show up around us is that we are always keeping thoughts around us from the past. Those thought-habits are to keep us safe, to make sure people think well of us, to ensure we can control the world around us.

All those reasons are bogus.

Because the World around you is exactly what you think. Exactly.

Worrisome thoughts create worry and anxiety around you. Fearsome thoughts create more fear. Angry thoughts create more anger. Look around you and you'll see this is true. Someone loses their temper – and suddenly everyone around them is a little more angry, or a little more fearful.

But the reverse is also true. Someone coming into a room with a big smile and lots of great things to say about everyone around them cheers everyone up.

Your thoughts – and the actions these spark – create the world around you.

The trick then, is to get control over your thoughts. Now, in "Go Thunk Yourself", I cover in some detail how various scientists have shown that you can change these mental thought habits by around 30 days of practicing a specific pattern of thinking – and that you can change your attitude just by putting a smile on your face – William James pointed this out around a century ago, and Plato way before that.

More recently, I stumbled upon the Levenson releasing techniques, and found an even simpler way to eliminate those nagging worries, fears, frustrations, etc.

You can actually and effortlessly be happy, peaceful, calm, and act with complete courageousness every single second of the rest of your life. Sure, it takes some work, but it can be done.

Which way would you rather live your life?

Lester Levenson and the 7th step of releasing

I don't know why, but you don't find this 7th step of the releasing technique mentioned in the various Larry Crane and Hale Dwoskin work-ups.

Practically, it's been around as a practice since time immemorial.

Here's what Levenson said in a tape series called, "The Way":

> 7. **Make your behavior that which a Master would do.**
>
> *Whatever you do, do it successfully.*
>
> *The more imperfectly we work, the lower down the scale we are.*
>
> *The action required to go free is releasing all the obstruction.*

A Master, as we've covered elsewhere, is someone who has already achieved a high state of enlightenment and self-knowledge. And there are more around on this planet than we consider. But that's in an earlier part of this book.

For our use here, it is really that one sentence and the explanation I pulled from his tape – not an exact quote, but close.

People have often used others' examples to compare and contrast their own lives with. Levenson is telling you to simply do what a Master would do.

Of course, you probably have heard that phrase, "What would Jesus do?" – which is completely applicable, just as "What would Buddha – or Lao Tse, or Confucius, or Muhammad, or any other major spiritual leader – do?"

The idea that comes to me, particularly in following Levenson's example above, is that you always work for perfection in every single thing that you do. All actions are professional and give a much greater value than are asked for. Wallace Wattles covered that exact point in his "Science of Getting Rich." Similarly Earl Nightingale covered similar points in his "Strangest Secret" recording.

And so very interesting was a point I first ran into from Napoleon Hill's "Think and Grow Rich" – where he quotes the psychologist William James – that all you have to do is to act the part and whatever you do will take the place of any feeling you are currently experiencing. Be brave, and you are. Laugh, and then you'll certainly be merry.

So that gives us a very practical and pragmatic approach to life. Study up on the lives and teachings of these spiritual leaders – or any Master in any field – and you'll see exactly how to approach life from that viewpoint.

Don't assume their persona, be your self – but make your *actions* those a Master would do. In other words, take all this in advisement, but throw it away if it doesn't let you be yourself.

Because you are already a Master, we are just working out how to let your inner light shine – aren't we?

Try this for 30 days and you'll start replacing habits you didn't even know you had.

And as I write this, I can already see where I can get some more improvement out of this – I hope you have as well.

Getting Your Life in Order - Cleaning Your Room

All life revolves around order, prediction, simplicity.

And while I've started revolving my own life around the Levenson releasing technique – amalgamating this into the earlier studies I started so long ago with "Go Thunk Yourself" – there are always so many lessons to find just in living.

The most recent one is that you really want to rid your life of things you are wanting to control, needing to approve, or that require your security. It isn't enough just to release on how these are affecting you – there's also where you are still working to do these on/for others.

These type of scenes are just holding you back.

Of course, this goes back to that 7th step of releasing - living your life as a Master would (which just brings out your own native Master abilities, doesn't it?)

So you can take any of the historical Masters who have lived among us (and some say still do) – or just look within yourself to see how you would like to be treated.

It's that easy. If you are involved in some sort of continuing mess where you feel you have to control someone else's actions or activities, then maybe it's time to let that go. It might mean you don't have to deal with those people any more.

But it will mean that your life gets more direct.

And, like cleaning your room, if you start doing this on a regular basis (as I advise getting your releasing going on a continuous basis), then your life becomes simpler and simpler. You live with far less effort. Which then means that magic and miracles become more and more commonplace.

There's far more about what Lester wrote that needs study and reflection. And I'm sure I'll be continuing this as I move to other projects and blogs about them. For me, those are easy subjects to talk about, much more rewarding than other areas.

But try this out for yourself and see if these make sense. See if you can't work at getting your own life more direct by seeing what complicated subjects you can just drop out of your active life.

How You Can't Win Them All, and Why You Shouldn't Try

While you can and should be willing to help everyone around you – and the Golden Rule says that you almost have to – don't expect that the world is going to immediately turn right around and give back.

There are people, sad as it seems, who are bound and determined to simply continue destroying everything and everyone around them in their way along their own little personal path to self destruction. These are the truly insane among us.

It's not that they can't be helped. Or that they can't get better. Or that they can't actually resolve to improve their lives and eventually find their own route and way to personal enlightenment. They are right now hell-bent on wrecking their own lives, which also then affects how they see and treat people around them.

So you have to be willing to "cut your losses" at some point and move these people off your lines. Actually, they will move off yours if you just let them. I think I've gone over this point before of realizing when you're fighting something and directly quit that action. Like finding out that you're beating your head against a wall – the pain is remarkably lessened when you stop.

At one point I'd been involved with ripoff artists for the around 2 years and finally got enough sense to just quit. It was that easy. They actually wanted away from me almost as much.

For them, it was like a tar baby they couldn't get unstuck from (Uncle Remus – Brer Rabbit – Song of the South). I was trying to get them Justice and help them as much as I could. But all my lectures were going on deaf ears. And when I finally saw their view of life, I could understand why they weren't listening – their view of life was that everyone was out to scam them, so no one was able to be trusted.

They are actually in a state of constant denial of the world around them. They are actually fighting everything that they encounter – scamming is their only defense, since the world is out to get them. If there's a brick wall anywhere near them, they can't wait to butt their head up against it. They can't get away from the ego-trap of making money with Other People's Money – yours. Their "work from home" business opportunities are just a second, low-paying wage-slave job. And now you're working for your credit card companies, too.

But this is just to tell you that you can get these guys off your lines more easily than you think possible.

Again, the Levenson releasing technique comes to view as a tool. The direct steps I use to continually apply this in my life are

1. *Look over and confront what is in your life – all thoughts and feelings*

2. *Accept any part of this (or all of it) that you can.*

3. *Simply let it go.*

Of course, life gets easier and more delightful as you do this. You enjoy life more and your feelings become more intense. You appreciate things around you much better. Abundance, good health, great relationships – all these become common place when you use the releasing technique.

You want to use Levenson's releasing techniques continually in your life. And in doing so, you can achieve incredible states of calmness – beyond any meditation – that will take you through anything life has to offer. Ultimately, it can take you into realms most humankind doesn't get a chance to visit often and where few are able to remain.

But that's a story for another time.

Right now, just help everyone you can, even those who don't want your help. But quit fighting anything and everything.

Simply let go of all your "wanting to sort it out" and stuff like that. Invest in everyone around you, but particularly those who want to invest in themselves.

People have to make (or find, actually) their own Peace. Some, sadly, aren't actually headed anywhere near that direction.

So let them go – right out of your life. They aren't looking for you – they're looking for people just like them.

But realize that you did make an impression on them, if only slightly.

And be thankful for the true friends you are finding in greater and greater number around you. Because that is what you are attracting with your releasing.

How Can "What am I" Achieve My Personal Freedom?

To answer this question, you have to drop using the mind. The mind is really only composed of thoughts. Thoughts are simply collected solutions to problems in the past – hoping that we might run into that problem in the future and have a ready answer to use.

But our mind can't really answer a question. It only poses more questions and analysis and reaction about the original thought – so that thinking is just a series of thoughts strung together in loose association. Unless you think in disciplined patterns, (force your mind to think in a concentrated approach) your mind winds up with thoughts widely different from what you started out.

Extreme examples of this are called, "scatter-brained" and also "paranoid-schizophrenic".

Concentration on a single thought is a time-honored tradition of stilling the mind. And practically, it was the only way to do so before release technique came about.

Concentrating on a particular question or situation allows the mind to still and the answer to come from the Universal. We've covered before about how we are all connected and our thoughts are sent out constantly – well, when you still your mind, you are able to get any answer to any situation or problem you have.

(Again, reject this completely and see if it isn't true for yourself. For all you know, you are being scammed right now. Check it out and see for yourself.)

Napoleon Hill gave an example of Dr. Gates, who would sit in a darkened room with a pad of paper, pen, and the nearby light switch. Gates would only concentrate on what was known about the problem at hand. Once he started getting answers, he would turn on the light and start writing as fast as he could to get it all down. Gates had a huge number of patents on file and was constantly in demand as a consultant to the major corporations of the day.

Meditation is often best done with a single question in mind. Concentrating on that will often give faster results than simply sitting in silence for the same period.

Now, combining a single, concentrated attention on a particular question in alignment with continual releasing of all random thoughts, a calm mind – this allows you to go behind the mind to get the answers from the Universal. The mind doesn't give answers, it gives back recordings of earlier solutions to similar problems. It will take credit for the answers which come – but those answers come from the Universal, not the mind.

The mind is only a pile of *recordings*.

The Universal stores all knowledge and is a font of *understanding*.

And once you answer that question, "What Am I?", then you have a grip on that Universal which will never let go.

But don't take my word for it. Try it for yourself.

The Fiction of Death and Living - it's only Love

Like Living, Death is a fiction – a dream – the Maya/Illusion we are all participating in.

Consider this logic, if you will:

We are all connected, the world is what we believe it to be. Those, of course, come from the very old "Huna" philosophy. And the word "philosophy" itself goes to "Love of what works."

Charles Haanel covered Love as a primal force, meaning that it exists and creates the world around us. Factually, and by extension, we are all Love at our base.

Lester Levenson's big breakthrough – the one which saved his life – was recognizing that Love works best on an out-flow. The more you love others is what brings more peace into your own life.

And this is the unconditional love you can find in pets and the saints.

"Sin" is yet another fiction, developed (like "Money") to improve the control, security, and approval desires. These in turn are based on denial of this central concept that there are no limits, denial that we are all connected and part of a greater whole. Huna shamans (kahuna's) had a harder time helping ha-oles (non-natives) just because so many of these imports brought with them the false data and beliefs that a person could harm another. And so would then tell the petitioner to go and "make amends" as they felt best, then come back to do the next step. Max Freedom Long tells about this in his "Secrets Behind Miracles".

So where to people go when they die? Nowhere – and everywhere. Because death is neither an end nor a beginning. I ran across an old Serge Kahili King article recently where he mentioned that an old tradition held that Living was just a dream – that when you "died" you simply woke up to another dream.

Dreams, of course, are another fiction – including the one you are "living" right now as you read this.

All there is, is Love.

Now some Eastern philosophies, and Levenson found these to explain what he had gone through, hold that God is within all of us and we are all part of God. Of course, you'll see the New Thought understanding there – but you will also see that while Alan Watts tells about this concept being integral to Zen Buddhism, it is also in the teachings of Jesus the Christ.

Of course, this makes sense again, since God is Love.

So you have to learn (or unlearn) to love death.

Because, like any good story, it pulls you along the plot line. Where that analogy fails is that this is a story which has no beginning and no end. Sleep is really an artificial end and beginning point of every day – and the enlightened have traditionally found that sleep was another fiction, that in higher states it wasn't necessary.

But this very fear of death is what drives so many of us. Levenson found that this was the arch-angel he feared through his own life. And brought him to the very real point where his doctor told him he had days, maybe as much as three months to live – only if he went to bed and didn't get out of it.

He really found out (since he still had a very active mind and drive to understand) that he had brought this on himself. In doing so, all that introspective analysis took him right out the top and into an unreality with the world around him. It took him 18 years and moving to seclusion in Sedona before he could figure out what he had done in order to talk to other people about it effectively enough to help them achieve that state for themselves.

I am still on this "path" to resolving this for myself. And you'll see the fallacy of that statement – it is really that I am awakening ever more slowly from the fictions I have accepted on how to live and exist.

By the same token, you can see why I tell you to learn from these other Masters as well (Napoleon Hill, Charles Haanel, Wallace Wattles, Earl Nightingale, Serge Kahili King and Max Freedom Long) – as these all studied widely and consolidated what they understood into simple and practical philosophies anyone could apply for themselves.

Each of these found very successful lives – and succeeded exactly to the same degree that they helped others with their own success.

That explains the fiction of Death. Because as we are all connected, our success depends on others' success.

Now, my living on a farm brings me into a quite different, less sheltered view of death. Farming is surrounded by the challenges of growing things and harvesting. Plants, like wheat and rye, are planted in the fall only to "sleep" during the winter and then rise tall in the spring to "die" about June where their seed can be harvested. If you don't harvest the seed, it plants itself to grow again the next year. Cows live longer lives in general. But you have to weed out your stock much as you weed a garden – otherwise, there isn't enough food for all of them and they will all suffer. Cows live, on average about 12-14 years (hardier breeds live longer). But like dogs and cats, they live shorter lives than humans (who live much shorter lives than some trees like the Burr Oak, which can exist for more than half a century). So just in day-to-day living on a farm you see death on a daily basis – if only in the insects making their way around.

And I would invite anyone to arrange their lives so that they can spend a few months or years doing nothing but communing with Nature. And taking that time to look within and find your Self, to really look at what is, to welcome this illusion around us and learn to appreciate it for what it is.

Because the truth and peace you seek is already present. You only have to quit pushing it away or saying it's not there.

Freedom Is (period.) - 130

Death is only one manifestation of your own self-imposed limits. I hope you enjoy finding others.

What is Your Path - How do You Find Your Way?

One key point has to be covered here.

Your path is entirely your own. There is only one Way for you – and that is the one you pick out and resolve for yourself.

This idea of using the releasing technique to get everything you really want in life – that doesn't work for everyone.

There are exactly as "many paths up the mountain" as their are individuals in this Universe. There can be no "one way and only one way" – because we are all connected, but completely different.

While all spiritual paths are correct in their basic data, many religions (and governments) go astray because they inherit the same problems their followers have. They think they are separate from everyone else and so they are right and everyone else is wrong.

Needless to say, this doesn't work. Thinking someone else is wrong just comes back to you, doesn't it? Accepting people for what they are, giving them unconditional love – these actions will bring you acceptance and love in return, won't they?

That old Golden Rule scene we've talked about over and over.

The other phrase I'm fond of quoting goes: "No one school has all the teachers." That's from the older Polynesian sayings, which are probably the oldest surviving philosophic system that this planet has. And those islands are amazingly peaceful these days.

While I tell people that releasing is probably the greatest discovery since Fire and the Wheel (right up there with sliced bread and spreadable margarine) – I also have to say that it's not for everyone.

I tell you to throw away all that you've read here and prove it for yourself. That is really, really the only way to find Truth.

Because truth is completely personal to you. No two people share the same exact truth.

Of course that explains why no government really works and dictators seldom end their career alive and in power.

The best approach is and always has been to let people work things out for themselves. Let communities solve situations as best they can, groups of communities decide what's best on a broader basis, states to solve solutions based on a broad consensus (if at all) and the national government to simply keep its nose out – excepting only national concerns like defense and safeguarding trade lines.

Every single government employee at all levels could release on having to control and approve anything for the rest of us, as well as only doing those things which would benefit others as they would like to be benefited. But they'd have to quit thinking and start looking to a greater power for solutions outside themselves . Don't hold your breath waiting for this to happen any time soon...

But regardless of politics and government, just work out the optimal solution for yourself.

Whatever your path is – go at it until you achieve your own personal Freedom and everlasting Happiness. We all share one other, common thing – inside, we are all Masters. And we just need to let is shine out through all that we've stacked up on top of it. Do just that for yourself and we all win.

Thanks for listening to all I've said here. Now I'm done.

You can safely throw it all away and write your own book now.

I wish you a great eternity.

So Now You Know Your Path - What's Next?

Of course, I've been having quite some fun applying what I laid out at the beginning of this, but there's one more update.

Mostly, just working on stilling the mind has done wonders. But the 1-2 punch of releasing any thought that comes in, followed by asking, "What's that thought coming from?" took me right back to "What am I?"

And that has produced the best results.

While I can't say that the mind is completely stilled all the time, I am having wider and wider gaps in time where there are no thoughts and I can just simply enjoy a very peaceful existence, just "Being the Witness" as Levenson covered so often. Because when you still the mind, in my experience, there's not much choice or reason to do anything else.

It's just natural.

And so this is what is bringing this concept I had earlier of "Intuitionist Living" or "Intuitionist Life". The explanation of this is that you really only live that type of life naturally – but your own thoughts take you out of it and make you effort at any decisions or planning you "have" to make. These "now-we're-supposed-to's" and "musts" and "have-to's" are all really fiction.

They only exist in a very busy mind. Quiet the mind, even a little bit, and their force weakens. Life becomes a calm, peaceful existence. (Or at least more calm and more peaceful.)

The intuitional and inspirational insights which start arriving (no longer relegated to pushing through as thought) are fascinatingly simple and direct. There's no question about them, no rush. There is a great deal of certainty accompanying them – but no dire urgency for them to happen.

I'm sure that if I were in a very action-oriented situation, I'd have faster and more immediate intuitions about what to do next.

But the flow of life is fascinating, even at this fairly low level. I'm sure that as I get used to it, all of this will seem commonplace after awhile. And there will be another, higher level to attain which seems uniquely interesting at that point.

So, as usual, throw this away and forget I ever said anything down this line. If it's useful to you, fine. Certainly, your mileage will vary. Definitely.

But I'm certainly having fun with this and thought to let you know.

Part III – Freedom Summary and Action Steps

In this book, I've perhaps covered entirely too much material. But this is the point – to give you plenty of stuff so that you can choose and develop your own path to personal Freedom.

This was originally a review of my "Go Thunk Yourself" self-help success book. I wanted to revisit what I had done 10 years before and update all this material with what I've found since.

While I've said it again, I have to apologize for all the writing I've done. This book was never necessary. As you reach your high state for yourself, this is obvious.

All this book contains is just a very workable path that I created for myself, based on research that I found useful. And it's tailor-made for me – one size doe not fit all; your mileage will very definitely vary.

This last section of the book is to help you determine what guru's coaches, books, materials, or whatever it is that you may seem to want to help you with your own search, your own patch construction. It's composed, again, of online essays I'd written to sort out the dross from the vital, the gold from the flim-flam.

It's you who will have to be the final judge as to whether this book or any essay in it is workable or useful for your own personal improvement or development efforts. For at this writing, I am hard at work simply applying all this stuff – and it may or may not take a few more months or years before I consider that my path is walked.

This book, however, is supposed to be about you – and not about me. And if *you* were wanting a sequence of steps and sequences on what to do – how would a person approach this?

The key point I've uncovered overall is that Levenson's releasing technique is an undercut to every type of self-help philosophy and practice out there. It only makes whatever author you are reading work even better. Whatever you are doing, releasing as you go simply makes it all much better, more effective.

There are probably two approaches to this:

1. Skip around this book and read what gets your interest. Then apply this to your life and see it it help you improve your situation.

2. Study this in the sequence as presented, applying it as best you can while you go along, then revise your sequence of actions with the new material you find.

Either of these is correct – or even a combination of them. It's also perfectly OK to just put this book on a shelf for later, or just give it away to someone else.

If you haven't run into this already – every thing that you do is perfectly OK. It's your life, live it however you want.

The reason I wrote this was not to point out any particular character flaw or limitation you might have – quite the reverse. You are already a perfect being – and are already enlightened. This book is only a way of giving you data you may or may not have encountered or figured out for yourself. I just want to help you become even more perfect in living the life that you have in front of you.

One workable approach

1. Read through (or simply scan) the book and see what you want to come back to and study more thoroughly later. Make notes in the margin, add tabs, dog-ear the pages.

2. Make a short list of things you'd like to improve in your life. You can change this as much as you want later. You just want a record of where you were when you started.

3. Now, come back and set a certain time each day - in a place and time you won't be disturbed - to both study some more of this book and put it to use in your life. Work out activities which you can then prove to yourself whether what you just read was workable for you.

4. As you finish off the book, compare notes with where you are now and see if you've either acquired, achieved, or accomplished some of that list. Look to see if you are now more active, or if things are easier and more effortless now. Look at your own beingness and see if you have more certainty or better self-esteem.

5. Start over with your scheduled study and now work over how you can apply each and every datum of this book. This time, if you have questions about the material, get the books or look them up online so you can see the original materials this book was derived from. Most of them can be gotten for little cost, or the time you spend downloading these. But where you have the physical book to hand (or the CD or DVD) you'll see that this is easier to study and cross-reference.

6. Once you get to the end of this third time through, check out your life at that point. Do you have more? Do you do more, are you still more active and effortless? How's your self-confidence and love for those around you?

7. Then, review this book (and the additional references you've collected as part of this study) once a month or so to keep you on the track you set for yourself. You'll find that your understanding has improved, that you have many more lessons to learn in your life.

Daily Schedule

Many people have found that some simple structure in their lives helps to make the changes they want.

a) Get a certain place and time to do your studies. Some location you won't be disturbed.

b) Schedule out studying these materials – or other related materials of interest.

c) Listen or read inspirational or motivational materials every day. This can be at this time, or in addition – such as a daily commute to a job.

d) Work at maintaining a calm, even approach to life during your day. Nightingale had this as a "calm, cheerful optimism". Levenson had this as courageousness, acceptance, and peace. Live from this level, and release anything that comes up which tries to knock you off this level.

e) Get the new mental habit of releasing constantly. Anything that comes up – just let it go. Keep working at this until your mind is quiet, your inspirations are instantaneous, and your own world is at peace regardless of what happens in the world around you.

f) Then answer "What am I?" (if you haven't already...)

You'll see Freedom showing up around you in incredible amounts. Your Happiness, your Joy – all the Peace you could want is already within you. It's always been there. You've only needed some help to allow yourself to just let it out again.

What do you do after this? Anything you want. It will be an interesting, new way of living. One you haven't experienced in some time. I can't tell you what you are going to want to do at that point. No one else other than you can, actually. Because you are going to be a different person at that point. All the masks you have been wearing, all the different habituated responses which you considered "normal" have been gone for some time. What you'll see now is your own, native Self.

Believe it or not, there's even steps beyond that to take. But you'll know what to do at that point – and will need no book or recordings or videos to tell you what you have to do next.

And I wish you all the speedy progress you could want for yourself. For up ahead is something very new compared to how you've been treating yourself all this time.

It's not the Future. It's a better Now. It's *your* creation – just as you've been doing all along.

The Key Data Behind Valid Self Help Books and Materials

Of all the work I've done to date, this is perhaps the most important – and potentially the most damning.

None of this is an easy walk in the park. But it is vital that I tell you at this point.

There are a handful of metaphysical principles which all successful self help programs contain. I've already gone over a checklist to see if any particular self-help guru isn't delivering the goods. So now I hope to tell you what they do need to contain.

1. **"Thoughts create your reality."** See Huna principle 1, Earl Nightingale's "Strangest Secret", Napoleon Hill's "Think and Grow Rich", Haanel's "Master Key System", etc.

2. **"You can connect to a Higher Intelligence/the Universal to get answers and intuitive suggestions."** See Haanel, Hill (Chapter 14), most religions and philosophies cover this point. The Silva Method.

3. **"Self inspection and personal analysis is your real path – if you need one."** This is the key point to Buddhism, especially Zen. As well Jesus gave many examples of his own meditating in the wilderness. Lester Levenson's release technique.

4. **"Your persistence and faith determine your progress toward enlightenment."** See Hill's talks on "Burning Desire", and other New Thought authors' comments on concentration.

Now you will also see that they have a set of programmed steps to follow, but any system being sold or promoted right now have these, so that's a given. This separates real self-help from poetry or artwork or mere "inspirational quotes".

When you get down to the bottom-line basics, you'll see that the *real* push and drive is to get the individual up to the point where they can let their *own* abilities shine out and manifest. It is at that point where anything they could need or want simply shows up around them. All these other goals work are just the process of getting them confident in their own abilities so that they can and will – on their own.

These four points above are the common theory points which have to be present for any real self-help progress to be made. If they don't tell you these points pretty quickly, you don't have a path to follow – except to keep paying their salaries with your "donations."

But money is another trap and only useful as an introduction to the broader subject of self-actualization.

It's whether they actually tell you that self-actualization is possible which will tell you their intent. And then you will know everything about them.

- - - -

Oh, and if you find someone who isn't searching, who is completely calm and at peace with everything – and while meanwhile being quietly confident of themselves enough to be only interested in you and the people around them – realize you just met one of the real, rare, genuine articles. Treasure them and help them as you can. Don't try to keep up with the help you'll be getting from them, because they really and factually only exist to serve.

Those are the real deals. About one in ten million or more. Cherish them. And learn so you can "do greater things than these."

What Makes A Self Help Guru Really Successful?

Unfortunately, most of these guys and their marketing firms have this backward.

You only have to study my Scam-Free Book and the Preamble to Covey's 7 Habits to find out why:

Most guru's and "success coaches" are out there to *sell benefits*.

They can and will give you a dozen solutions to any want or need you think you have. But Covey found in his study of a couple hundred years of success material in the U.S. – that the last 50 years were devoted to just attitude adjustment *instead of actually working out the underlying causation and eradicating it.*

Of course, I did my own study and completed most of it before I found Covey's work as a side-check on that research. I only took dead authors whose works were still being widely circulated, then looked for commonalities (crossovers) in them.

This wound up in my "Go Thunk Yourself" series.

But as I knew in follow-up research that something was missing. And only found that recently.

And in reviewing all this for my last book in this area then brought up the fact that I pull my own success from a wide-range of material – but only four main subject areas.

The point today is to cover how you can tell a real deal from a fake.

I mention (probably too much) that you need to be familiar with Maslow, Cialdini, and Levenson to know that you are scam-free (see the book on this, as well as the scam-free checklist).

While a scammer and an honest practitioner can be separated by finding their actual intentions (but you still can't separate them from their money, different than the fools they ply) –

even the people having great financial success in their marketing may not understand what they actually need to do to be the "real deal."

1. Real guru's aren't concerned with themselves as an example. The best will actually try not to bring their own successes up, since this then builds resistance by giving you a "hidden standard" to measure your own progress against.

2. Real guru's are interested more in your self-actualization than anything they say or do – or even in the materials they offer. ("...ye shall do even greater things than these...") They aren't just offering to help you cure physical ailments, get rich quick, have an incredible sex life, or "attract" that luxury car/huge house/expensive trinket you've "always" wanted?

3. There is no dogma or hyper-compartmented teachings to swallow wholesale. Real teachers will insist that you work this out for yourself and only accept something if and when you've proved it for yourself.

4. And while it's necessary to "make money" to survive in this culture, it's more to the point that people won't value something unless they have to contribute something first or as a result. Money, especially hard-earned income, is one way to do this. CEO Space requires people to go out and learn by getting people to get investors contributing to their success.

And so this really gives you a four-point checklist to see if you have a fake or the real deal in front of you:

- Look up their website and see if it's personality and approval-driven. Does it have a lot of pictures of the principles with other celebrities?

- Do you have to buy extensive packages of materials which can only be used under certain conditions and agreements? Are you forbidden from improving on these materials or teaching your own version?

- Are these guru's and their staffs only really interested in how you are progressing with these materials? Do they give you a testimonial form to fill out? Or are they simply giving you solutions to insatiable desires – how rich is rich?

- Are you constantly being asked for more money every time you turn around. This can also be insidious, as they are putting pop-ups on their site to get you to sign up for their email course – then claiming they have XXX,XXX subscribers or "millions of satisfied customers worldwide!"

Now, take it as a given that since the vast majority of people on this planet are running on 95% subconscious habits, you are going to attract people into a real self-help study which can let them achieve enlightenment only by first telling them that "your lumbosis can be easily alleviated with high-powered and unique methods we have." As well, that they can "live more abundant and prosperous lives" if they start doing such-and-so at such-and-such price per hour. Only when you tell them that *the reason they want all these things also has to be addressed* – that is the first time you are bringing up the point that self-actualization is the higher goal to *really* shoot for. Because only when they've had success in dealing with these relatively minor problems of having abundance or happiness or good health in their lives (which are actually native to everyone anyway) will they be able to see that there is something higher that they can and should be reaching for.

The final point – *do they deliver the goods*? Some certain fields of study have the problem of having promised their people that they can attain super-high personal states, but not having those actual courses and processes available for purchase at any prices. Zen Buddhism says at least that while many people have become bodhi/achieved satori, others might take several lifetimes before they do – while some can get there in minutes, per Alan Watts. When you study up on a self-help guru, look to see if they are delivering a finite set of goods that is here right now.

If they are just selling you the "next great thing" with no end in site – realize you are their income source. And little else. Move on. Find yourself another guru, or become your own.

Hope this helps.

Personal Improvement Crossovers and Compartments

All life, at least our humankind version of it, is severely compartmented. People live their lives in cloistered cubicles, even when they are right next to a person. Each of us lives very unique experiences – so much so that when a set of witnesses watch an accident happen, no two people have the same report.

And we keep our knowledge and our beliefs running in this same manner. Sciences are kept uniquely different in different fields. Medicine is even more refined – specialists for everything. Cancer treatment is by area of the body, not by type of cancer. (Even though all cancer has commonalities of causation and treatment.)

So we can take this to extremes, and live very individuated lives. It's even remarkable nowadays when people share the same thought simultaneously. Or have pets who "know" when you are sick or feeling down. People who are "empathetic" are valued highly.

But to study ancient philosophies and religious texts, our modern world is the anomaly. These books and scrolls and verbal traditions tell us that we are all connected. All interconnected. We can actually find out anything we want to whenever or wherever we choose.

Quantum Physicists have been some of the first scientists to discover this – that the presence of the operator causes the outcome of the experiment, no matter how well shielded. And so many of these have gone back to study philosophies, especially ancient Eastern texts, in order to understand what they had just ran into.

This is another indicator of scam or fraud – when they won't let you look at other data. Wide open studies like Huna tell you to use any part or all of what you find workable for yourself and improve on it or combine it with other studies. Corporations like Scientology tell you not to "mix practices" and that studying related fields or authors is "squirreling". (While Hubbard himself crafted his work based on a wide variety of texts ranging from Aleister Crowley and Qabalah to Psychology and "past life regression". He then called these by his own nomenclature and slang, creating his own ivory tower you weren't supposed to step foot out of.) It's no small wonder that Scientology has long had the moniker of "cult".

Internet Coaching and Marketing guru's have this same problem. Once they train people to get out on the Internet for themselves, their consumers will find that they don't have all the answers and then leave – and might even demand their money back. (The most petulant of these can't stand to be blogged about, either.)

But the answers to any questions can be found simply when you look for crossovers from other fields.

The more I look for answers, the more I find. As long as you keep a truly open mind and are testing everything you find for workability, you find amazing material that can radically improve your life. You'll also find where studies and systems are missing huge chunks which would make them more workable.

My own results in looking for crossovers lead me to the four core studies which interacted as a "tetrad" and would result in real increase of personal ability, prosperity, and freedom: Huna, Silva Method, Levenson Release Technique, and New Thought bestsellers.

I invite you to study these four resources and find the crossovers for yourself – not just to accept what I say here.

And I can only tell you that by being truly open to the world around you, and seeing it for what it is – not what you think it should be or would like to change it into – only then will you see a remarkable world around you and be able to take advantage of the vast amount of opportunities ever present.

4 Goals to Achieve which will Save Your Life and Everyone Else as well

I tend to learn from my "dreams", even when it's the one we share in living in this Universe.

And last night was a doozy. But what came from it is that when you release on goals in order to achieve them, you are actually helping everyone around you as well. So the bigger the goal, the more you help humankind in general.

Meaning, that if you really have concern for this planet and the people on it, you'll work on releasing the biggest goals you can dream of. We are all connected, after all.

These four goals (word them as you like):

- World Peace
- Abundance for every single person
- Ecological balance
- Personal Freedom for every single person

Now, I could tell you more about these (and have, in my various blog posts over the years), but the key point is that you need to deal with individuals to get this to work. Never, ever, the government. Because the government (like money) is a fiction, a contrivance and as you release more and more, it becomes obvious that people only use the concept of government to control, to gain approval, and to provide a false sense of security.

The next point it is that you never "fight" anything. That also doesn't work. You become the thing you are fighting. In order to dissolve a situation, you will need to simply welcome it and release it. Recognize it for what it is and let it go. It will then cease to have any effect on you. If you do need to do something, you'll get the intuitional inspiration of what to do. Don't "think" about it – just put it into motion.

As you start working on these broad goals to release, then you'll see how they interact, as well as other reasons you need to work on all four. Time permitting, I'll set these each up with the data I have and help you as possible with your own work.

4 studies to learn from

My own background, as I've said, came from Scientology – although I don't use anything I learned there anymore. It was a great introduction to a wide world of philosophers, religious prophets, and spiritual guides, but it's a limited study.

When I started butting up against the limits of that subject, I started studying the core texts it was derived from. This lead to my "Go Thunk Yourself!" study, which lead me right into New Thought.

New Thought is a very wide umbrella which has incorporated a lot earlier philosophers, as well as the bulk of the really successful self-help books such as "Think and Grow Rich", "Science of Getting Rich", and "Master Key System."

Somewhere along those studies, I stumbled upon Huna. This is the oldest known surviving philosophy on this planet. And interestingly, owes its rebirth in popularity (at least in the Western world) to Max Freedom Long, who gave it it's name. (Practically, the subject was so immersed in the culture, that it didn't have a single name before that point, much like water has several names for its various forms.) Long was a New Thought student, but I found that out later.

The third study is Silva Method, after the work Jose Silva did in his life-long study of the human condition and how to improve it. This is very powerful stuff, more powerful than even its practitioners know. But in the last decade, they've seen how it's more broadly applicable than earlier known.

A fourth study is Lester Levenson's release technique. Also known as the Sedona Method. And there are other variants around – they all work. Larry Crane and Hale Dwoskin, as well as Stephen Seretan – all these have their own individual approaches, but they all trained directly under Levenson and so got the real scoop on how to help anyone achieve their own Freedom and Peace of Mind.

I use all four of these together as the most effective way to quickly resolve personal situations and problems in my life.

Any of them individually would take you right on out to enlightenment if you really, really studied and applied them. All of them can also be toyed with to simply make your life more comfortable.

My own use, with Haanel, Hill, and Wattles providing the theoretical base – is to use the Alpha centering technique of Silva to get into a high personal state in order to use Levenson's release technique to simply let things go. Huna provides the glue to hold everything together.

And I would tell you these four things:

1. Know we are all connected (7 principles of Huna).

2. Know how the universe works (New Thought authors as listed.)

3. Use Silva techniques to get into a personal high state of certainty.

4. Release with Levenson's techniques so that you drop the underlying desires which hold everything in place.

Where to get the data

I've worked to republish the key New Thought authors at my Go Thunk Yourself Bookstore (Lulu.com).

For Huna, I have Max Freedom Long's books there and also tell you to visit http://huna.org , where you'll see all Serge Kahili King's work. Tad James' work is also recommended.

While Silva has undergone many transitions since Jose passed on, I'd still recommend getting a copy of his Ultra-Mind CD's as you can. These I know give you all the data you need to get going. (I'll find you a good link for this.)

Levenson's original stuff is most easily found at Larry Crane's site. I've also found some original Levenson recordings on Hale's, but it's much harder to locate there.

Practically, all of the above is also released to the Internet in various forms. So if you can afford to spend the time and bandwidth, you can get this all for "free."

The key point is to get this data, get your self proofed up and doing well, then tackle the bigger issues we all face as part of humankind.

[An interesting note: you'll see in both of these sets that they line up more or less as "tetrads" - which you can find more about on my "Go Thunk Yourself, Again!" blog.]

An Apology for My Dreams and Yours

You see, this universe we live in is exactly backwards from what we have been taught and have accepted as true. I, as you, have been pushing down this line, hoping for better answers as we go along.

And as I've covered at various points, both Levenson and Huna hold that the world around us is a dream, an illusion, "Maya".

Anyone can start running into this as they start to work the top end of goals. While "having a nice car" or "having a loving relationship" are all very nice – you also have to recognize that you have also put "not having" as a goal much earlier than this and agreed to it as more powerful than anything else. Or you wouldn't have to now work at getting something to show up.

OK, back up: Levenson (and other ancient mystics and Masters) held that the being (meaning: "you" and "I") creates the world around them. This is, of course, the first principle in Huna – and covered in <u>Napoleon Hill</u>, <u>Earl Nightingale</u>, <u>Charles Haanel</u>, and a host of New Thought Authors. ("We become what we think about.")

Now, when you start working on goals, a lot of people (such as the example in Wattle's "Think and Grow Rich") work on getting *material things* to show up. This is also the basis of "The Secret" DVD, where people are being told how to "attract" things into their lives.

But the kicker is in the question, "Who is doing this attracting?" You then find out that the person is responsible for the Universe around them, that they put their own lack there first in order to solve it.

True.

Think it through for yourself.

It is not "you" and "the Universe". Haanel's whole "Master Key System" was a treatise on how you get up to the point that you figure out you put the whole thing there. Even Scientology's "secret end phenomenon's" all deal with this one point: taking complete responsibility for having "mocked up" or created the exact problem you are dealing with.

And Canfield as well as Levenson (and Hubbard) make a point that you have to take responsibility for what you are doing and have done in order to do something about it.

Or, you can directly release the goal you created originally which was contrary to it, plus the desire below it.

This now explains why Levenson pointed out to get beyond having to have "stuff" and simply get your Freedom instead. Otherwise all manner of dire catastrophes ensue.

Why is this? You wreck your own game. What's the point of having everything you could possibly want – if you have worked all this long time to make sure you *didn't* have it to begin with?

All philosophies (not necessarily the religions based on them) contend that you are an infinite being in your own right. "There are no limits." as Huna covers.

But that same statement says we are all connected. And this explains the world around us as we see it. It appears to be composed of multiple versions of reality, all mushed together for our own group amusement. It is the game we are playing.

And you can cease playing this game at any point. The trick is to make sure that you don't have to keep playing any game at all – or you'll just put the whole thing back again. And so the problem that many of the rich had – where they would go bankrupt over and over and over – only to just regain their fortune each time.

But you have to know that the fiction of Money is just another game. So is the fiction of Government.

All around you, every single little and big thing – is all Maya – Illusion.

And you get rid of small parts of it by doing Goals Releasing. Literally, you sit on your Butt and release the reasons you don't have something and then it shows up. This is Stephen Seretan's KISS (Keep It Simple, Sweetheart) method he got directly from Levenson.

This stuff is too easy. Let's lay it out:

1. Use Silva Method to "go to Level" and meditate at Alpha or Theta (or Delta, if you can). Get this as a constant "on" condition – practice staying at this state during your whole day and night.

2. Release everything that shows up, taking these down to basic and sub-basic desires. After you've been releasing constantly for awhile and get fairly imperturbable, give yourself some big goals, such as: "I allow myself access to Infinite Intelligence." or "I allow myself Infinite Beingness." All this does is set the stage for some massive realizations about how this universe around you works – and how you put it there to begin with.

3. Keep on going "all the way out" and don't let up for *any* reason. Want your Freedom more than you want this Maya around you. You want to move from Mystic (initiate) to Adept (master) – which is only a single release away. (Which explains how Alan Watts quotes an artist who said that the attainment of real Zen [an ultimate satori state] could take some people lifetimes and others just minutes. See the <u>Wikipedia article on Mysticism</u> to see what's possible here.)

And there is no 4. Because once you get to that point, you really do see that you are only attracting your own lack – that there is nothing "out there" except what you put there, or not.

This is why all these guru's and coaches are so very amusing. Because while they are all helping you improve your success, they don't take it all the way out. They keep telling you how to "pimp your ride", or telling you how to drive more safely, or evade the cops – instead of letting you in on the secret of teleporting.

(That secret, by the way, is the same as telepathy: distance, all Space and Time, are fictions. We are *all* already intimately connected in the Now. Release on *that*.)

While there are "many paths up the mountain," you'll also quickly see that there never was a mountain to begin with.

But you knew that.

Coda

Let me tell you about an interesting dream I had last night – a couple actually.

We aren't concerned about the details of them, as much as the lesson I took away from having them.

(And this won't probably make much sense until you read it through a couple of times. Mostly because the theory is very basic to how this world around us is set up.)

I.

The first was about two forces found in this frame of reference around us, called Altos and Menos. But you could call them about anything.

Both are Love-based.

- Altos = Love + Thought
- Menos = Love + Physical Universe

Altos speeds up manifestation/attraction/demonstration of anything you really want or seems important.

Menos slows these down.

Love in both cases is the creation element. Create your thoughts, or create more physical universe.

The trick is that the physical universe (and this is held by several different sources) is just composed of condensed thought. The more people agree something exists, the solider and more "real" it gets.

So these two aren't actually equally opposed or balanced. By withdrawing Love from either side, the force in that equation is withdrawn.

The bottom line is in who decides how much Love or Thought to put there.

This is Be – or Self. Be is what causes Love to exist or function. Be creates all thought.

You can simply decide at any point to change your mind. That changes the world around you.

II.

This second dream occurred earlier last night. Again, it doesn't really matter about the details. It matters about the principle below it.

In the military, this describes an interesting phenomenon called "short-timer syndrome." People agreed to fill out a contract (in the volunteer military, not the draft) for a certain amount of time. The closer they got to getting out (finishing their contract), the more light-hearted and unmotivated they became. All they had to do was to "stay out of trouble" and they were done. So they'd do what they had to to "get by" – and very little else. Their uniforms were perfect, their area neat and clean.

But nothing would really get done. And since they knew all the rules, you really couldn't catch them at anything. You'd simply go get someone else to do it. Because there was no way to really threaten them with anything – they would just put up with you for another few months and then they'd be gone.

But you, on the other hand, had a long career in front of you. You can be sent on long tours of duties in foreign lands without recourse. So you toe the line.

No one was going to cut orders for a short-timer to go anywhere – they'd just have to cut another set of orders to bring them right back...

III.

Anyone, at any time can get this "short-timer syndrome." It just takes realizing that the physical universe has no hold on you whatsoever.

You just have to cross that thin line which separates Being from Doing and Having.

To do requires some sort of playing ground. And to have requires you accumulate stuff on that playing ground.

But real Be – not the approval-oriented fiction, but real certainty of Self and the unflappable peace that comes with it – this is the point. When you quit associating your Self with a body or any specific identity in this playing ground we call the Physical Universe, then you have achieved that rare state called satori or enlightenment or illumination.

And it's just that simple.

This is the point of Dr. Hew Len's modern Ho'oponopono. This is the point to the Silva Method and Silva Ultramind. And even deeper, what Lester Levenson found when he discovered and developed the Sedona Method release technique.

For when you can't be controlled or need to control, when you don't need approval from anyone, when you are secure and safe regardless of the world around you (needing no physical situation in your life) – then and only then you have all the Freedom, Peace, and Joy you could ever want. And just slightly above that point: all the Peace of Mind you can handle and more.

All the self-help and personal development techniques will only take you so far. Right up to the brink, in fact.

But then you have to make the decision to step over that line.

Once you do, it's "all downhill" after that. Piece of cake. Easy rider stuff.

You'll find the personal meaning of "a peace that passes all understanding."

And resolving conflicts or troubles in this universe will become a detached hobby – if you want to go that route. When you get clear of all your own problems or wants or lacks (because you know you can create solutions any time you want) then it's moot whether you want to create and exert the energy necessary to do so.

Because you'll have all the Choice you could want after that point. You'll be at a permanent Zen state.

Now that doesn't mean you can't get all embroiled again in anything you choose. You created this world for yourself to begin with, after all. Just because you can be at that state all the time, doesn't mean you have to. It's a trade off.

But everyone should try it at least once in their lifetime.

The point is that it will be your conscious choice from that point forward.

IV.

From http://www.miraclesandinspiration.com/hooponopono3.html

> *Spirit, Superconscious, please locate the origin of my feelings, thoughts of (_____fill in the blank with your belief, feeling, thoughts_____).*

> *Take each and every level, layer, area and aspect of my being to this origin. Analyze it and resolve it perfectly with God's truth.*

> *Come through all generations of time and eternity. Healing every incident and its appendages based on the origin.*

> *Please do it according to God's will until I am at the present.*

> *Filled with light and truth, God's peace and love, forgiveness of myself for my incorrect perceptions.*

> *Forgiveness of every person, place, circumstances and event which contributed to this, these feelings thoughts.*

Additional Resources - Addenda

Basics of Releasing

This is just a record of the basics for you to refer to if you haven't done releasing before.

Actually, if you go to any of the various Levenson releasing technique sites, you'll find all the basics you could want. Additionally, you can get free downloads and materials, including CD's, which will cover this in far more detail and with examples.

The simplicity is just these two actions:

1. Accepting what is,
2. Letting it Go.

The ultimate goal is wanting Freedom more than you want the World. This will take you right on out to a high level of personal enlightenment.

As some had difficulty with this, the World was broken down into 4 singular "wantings" you use to relate with that World around you:

- Wanting Control
- Wanting Approval
- Wanting Security
- Wanting Separation/Oneness

The lower you go down the list, the deeper the level of the want.

The Wanting Control is often typified by frustration or impatience with people around us, as they simply aren't doing what we want them to do – or vice-versa. Like wanting a slow driver in front of you to speed up, for instance. Or talking to the TV and telling someone how they should change some behavior you noticed them doing.

Wanting Approval is a very common scene – popularity contests, or resentment at not being chosen for a team – any of these keep us stuck to behaviors where we are acting to please someone, or that we think others should get our OK before they do anything.

Wanting Security is far more basics. And needing to control or get approval is held in place by these. This unease is present with any time we are job hunting, or our position with a company or in life is threatened. Of course, this brings a lot more stress into our lives where we aren't in a peace-time activity. But it can also be the annoyance of a power outage, or bills you have to pay.

Wanting Separation or Oneness is ever present, but we are not usually aware of it. Wanting to be part of a group is of course a factor in wanting approval, but more basic. Wanting to "get away from it all" is the reverse – but is very basic. And might be the reason we have to have vacations at all. It's also the point of having people recognize your individuality.

There are definite feelings associated with all of these wants. As you start discovering these wants, you will see common feelings show up on certain ones. There may even be locations in the body where you have physical sensations when these feelings and wants occur.

Of course, use the below steps to release what you find as you find it. Practice will make this easier.

And remember – you can't do this wrong, you can't screw it up. No one is looking over your shoulder and giving you a grade on your performance. What happens when you release is only what happens for you. So be easy on yourself and do only what you can when you can. You'll make it eventually, regardless.

The six steps were revised from Levenson's own original series. But were changed only to make them more workable. Again, these are laid out in more detail through any of the various books and recordings you can find. Even videos online will explain these more.

The six steps are:

1. You must want freedom more than you want approval, control, security, or separation/oneness.

2. Decide that you can release in the moment

3. Notice what you are feeling in the moment, and determine which of the four wants underlies that feeling, and then let the feeling go. (But don't hold onto a feeling if it's already gone in order to determine what want was present.)

4. Release constantly, regardless of what you are doing or who you are with.

5. If you feel "stuck", then simply let go of that stuck-feeling, or wanting to change that "stuckness."

6. Every time you release, you will probably feel lighter, happier, and freer. Often you need to release on any exhilaration you feel – so you can keep releasing.

You can make a chart of the four needs and the six steps to keep in your wallet or purse or pocket – until you know them by heart and are able to release easily.

The idea is that you keep going with this line of practice until you can release instantaneously and near-automatically, any time you experience a negative or adverse feeling in your life.

Again, get the published material on this, or see some videos until these make perfect sense to you. You may even want to buy some of the intro materials or courses that these sites offer. Or attend seminars. What you do with this is up to you and what you want to achieve with your life.

Your Freedom Is.

Cults and Governments: Make Money and Prevent Freedom

(Note: this data is controversial and is mostly the opinion of this author. It is included for your use and application to the world around you. Of course, it may just give you something else to release...)

This may be best discussed as a complete theoretical concept – figuring that the people who read this will find it intuitively, all buried in some stretched mathematics. They'll skip down to the best part – and others who aren't ready won't see it at all, but just think I'm over the edge... Which I am, after all.

And this essay (as I posted it to a blog) is also kept overlong on purpose – just to show the point that most people won't actually use the data. The vast bulk of Internet users live on instant gratification and won't bother. Those who are willing to suspend disbelief and do the hard work of research to follow their heart – those are the ones who have that very tiny chance of making it.

It's not any government who is going to help you find your freedom. Nor any particular belief-system. Just you...

Natural Distribution, the Bell Curve, and Life

This is a natural distribution which you see in nearly everything around you. It tends to pull order from chaos if you can line up the data with the right comparative. (Told you this would get thick real quick...)

Now, any of these distributions has the 20/80 Pareto Principle in it, which then breaks down again around 2-4% on each extreme edge (20% of 20%).

The problem with philosophy and enlightenment is actually their continually reducing results, as these 2% limits continue to interact all the way along. These chain-react all the way up the line. Naturally.

Consider this natural distribution as showing how each level toward attainment works – only a very small handful in every "level" will actually achieve what they are seeking.

Levels of Enlightenment based on natural distribution

What is easily observable is that only a handful of people actually are successful in life. Earl Nightingale laid this out in his Strangest Secret – only 5% in that study were actually able to make a success out of life. Everyone else wound up either just "scratching by" or on the Welfare dole. Of course, these statistics were out of the 1050's, but these have been examined later and found to be the same percentages.

Between 2-5% actually make a successful life. (.02 chance)

Now, taking this on up, you'll then see that the really, extremely and outrageously successful people are just 2% (or so) of those. The very rich are just about 1 in 10,000 – or close to 2% of 2%. (.0004 chance)

On up from that are the very, very successful, or the uber-rich. These are about 1 in 100,000 or so. (.000008 chance)

And if you want to wind up on the richest person on the planet list, you are going to have to apply another 2% to that – about 1 in 10 million. (Giving you a .00000016 chance.)

This is what drives scams along. I was just talking with a former scam-coach (he found out he was working for scammers after he had been there for awhile and discovered their actual statistics.) He pointed out their business model actually consisted of finding and selling dupes a bill of goods which had them build their own ecommerce site. Only about 2-3% of these finished building their site. Another 2-3% of those actually made their original investment back. And out of that tiny amount, only about 2-3$ of those then made a real "killing" from whatever they chose. This last bunch are then interviewed in the infomercials, by scantily-dressed, over-buxom "hostesses".

This is also then the same control and approval methods which various companies use to get you buying their products and continuing to support their services. This is the phenomenon which makes "consumers" – which are literally "people who use it up" and customers, which are "creatures of habit". (But that is all covered in my online lesson series and book on how to scam proof your life.)

The deal is that they hype these "actual examples" to get you sold on the idea that you could do it. However, the FTC had to crack down on these, which would then tell you that the average results are in fact that you just lose money with these deals. Some to the tune of over $30,000...

Natural Distribution and Spiritual Enlightenment

Same goes for making "saints" out of "sinners." While both of those terms are inaccurate, they really give us the same points of digression people follow who are going to make their way out of this mess we call humankind existence.

The vast bulk of the people have no clue what's really going on. They live average lives going to work most of the week and paying out their income to support an average lifestyle, buying and paying off stuff that makes them feel secure. The government takes a huge chunk, as does their union (if they are in that shrinking minority), and more than half of what is left of what they make are sent to the black holes of insurance and finance companies. The average hard-working American, due to credit cards, usually has nearly nothing left to show for their life's work – which is the exact design of advertisers, finance companies, and any government.

Now, about 2-4% figure out that they can actually improve their lives. These are the people who buy self-help, spiritual, and personal development books/tapes/seminars. The bulk of everyone else gets by with going to church on a regular basis.

(The reverse minority are nihilists, who just consider life's all a loss and that it is basically pain.)

Out of those 2-4% who know there's a way out, only 2% of those will actually work out what their path needs to be in order to "go free" and "make it".

And only about 2% of those will then stick to it and follow that path.

But of those finalists, only 2% will actually get enlightened in a given lifetime. Or about 1 in 10 million. Most of these keep it quiet, so you don't hear much about them. (Follow the Christ's works and you'll see the problems he had with charismatic popularity and word-of-mouth advertising.)

That gives us a scale of:

  * The mundane "Muggles"

  * The Perceptive

  * The Genius

  * The Skywalkers

Now, the scale doesn't really quit there, but the levels above enlightenment can't be described in our words – they can only be intuited or imagined.

Churches, Self-Help Guru's, and Money

Now, this also explains why there isn't any money in philosophy and why real spiritual extremists (the guys who made it all the way out like Lao Tse (wrote Tao Te Ching), Siddhartha Gautama (Buddha), Jesus of Nazareth (the Christ) – none of these cared a hoot about money or even civilized society as it existed.

They were at or above that 4th level.

So in order to "do" anything with this metaphysical/spiritual stuff on a wide model – society wide – you have to have a lot of people working at the lower levels to keep people involved in it.

Not that this either makes or prevents people from achieving actual enlightenment – but it's a key point of having support groups for those who are between the 1st and 4th levels.

Any government, loosely defined, is a support group. Mostly devoted to the darker side of survival – but still, it supports those contributing to it (particularly those in power).

In all these, people pay their dues and follow along as best they can. They all know that if they keep to what they are seeking, they will find it.

Now, additionally, you won't find the uber-rich being the enlightened, either. They are still looking for themselves (or looking out for themselves.)

You see, once you get into the third level (Genius), money doesn't matter. You've got all you really need. And most of the reasons people have for keeping this fiction called Money going no longer apply to living – at least Genius' see it that way. If they need it, it's there. Otherwise, skip it – not worth investing the energy into it. Look up the lives of Sun Tzu, the Christ, and Siddhartha and you'll see they just skipped the whole idea of money and what it "can buy".

Genius live in the intuitional – everything gets provided at that level. But there's a curious caveat as well. Levenson pointed this out in the beginning of his "Fireside Chat" series, which Larry Crane published. When a person is getting everything handed to them, they have to keep going and move above that level. Or catastrophe happens. We saw this recently in one famed self-help guru who was in the middle of a process where he was pulling in around $400,000 – and some people died. Now he's charged with manslaughter.

You have to move beyond money or anything it buys, or any identification with a body – and that puts you into that next level, of real enlightenment (Skywalkers).

But there are people around these Geniuses who can "make money" off their existence and actions. And many who know that they have to keep this going in order for them to finish finding their own route to salvation, so they have to build churches and maintain followings in order to support their lifestyle. This doesn't say anything is bad about this, it's just a fact of life that "things" cost money. Especially if you don't get that you actually do make things show up around you – the money aspect is just a frivolous additional exercise. Like Wallace Wattles – what you need will show up for you along the existing lines of trade and manufacturing.

The Trick to Beating the Natural Distribution Curve and Achieving Enlightenment

The trick is that while there is a small minority of truly brilliant, there is also a minority of the equally-brilliant-but-criminally-destructive. And these two balance each other out. It's that old yin-yang thing. The middle route (quite Zen) is the way which actually wins out. The criminal are those who are really keeping this planet down. It's their offset which makes this distribution model the way it ends up. If there were no offset, we'd simply all go free in short order. And it's the fact that criminals just can't get it, so are always lop-sided and off-balance. Their base is destruction; they are always self-destructive to themselves and everyone around them.

But for all those people who are working as scammers and ignorant dicto-crats (North Korea, Uganda, anywhere people are being starved into submission) – mafia types which infiltrate (and run) governments – these are all equalized in the society as a whole, very effectively and at great expense, by honestly for-good-only organizations (Red Cross, among others) and everyone-wins, top-manager networks like CEO Space.

That's the real reason for support groups like churches, social networks, and clubs like the Optimists. They need your help to keep the balance.

It's our top minority (extremists) who are able to make it out in spite of. But you also see that the noise the lower end makes is what keeps the whole thing a mess – and so keeps this distribution pattern in place. So only the very few can make it out. (Now, eventually, it's possible for everyone to make it out – but that's a complete other story...)

[An interesting sidebar is that the "Middle Ground" is where the enlightened "sky-walkers" find themselves. To these, there is no "evil" and "good", but just the whole Zen experience. From that viewpoint, this whole essay is completely an excess. Listening to Alan Watts explains why and how this is.]

How to Get Yourself Enlightened is by NOT Going After It

Essentially, you can't get there from here.

Practically, the leap from Muggle to perceiving your own path out is as wide as perceiving there are geniuses and then becoming one. And the gap between an operating genius and becoming an enlightened sky-walker is even broader.

Again, there is a trick to this. This middle road can't be described in any of our languages. It can't be taught; it can't be studied. It has to be experienced, which is the way of all truth. You can't "work" at this, you can't pay anyone to help you achieve it. You can't stumble on this by accident (although there are plenty of serendipitous synchronicities to take advantage of — or not.) And when you know you're there, you are. Meanwhile, you simply know that something isn't complete, and so you are still looking...

So don't think I'm anything above being a genius. If I were, I wouldn't be writing this – it would just be obvious and not needing the telling. I can only tell you the apparent steps you might or might not take to get up to the level you can then make your own "leap of faith".

Route To a Top End?

Intuition and your own Imagination are apparently the only effective skills you can develop in order to get up to that point. At least the most effective known at this writing. You can derive such a path from studying as close as you can to what true Masters have said. But you have to listen to these with your heart.

The trick is to get beyond having to "know" what is going on. You have to get beyond knowing, and find your own intuitional sense.

Of course, this goes beyond printed matter – but you won't need it by this time, according to sources found to date. The Tao itself is a bit of a comic book, since it says that what can be spoken or written isn't the Tao – and then continues on to tell all about it...

This starts to explain some of what we are running into in trying to discover this path – and why it's so "hard" to do. Because you have to give up all the effort you're expending to find everything you've been looking for. (This is as it's really been there all along...)

Practically, you have to use whatever you are using to get enlightened to un-do their very fact and effectiveness of those exact tools. You won't need them after that point, anyway. The impossible first becomes possible, and then they both become the same.

Again, words fail here as a description. But the reason for this is because you don't need them any more. (And because this essay is of course supposed to be motivational, and get you to do something.)

You go to, and then beyond, the level of a Christ, a Buddha, a Master. There are obviously levels beyond just achieving the level of an enlightened being coexisting on this planet. Obvious.

- - - -

And we're going to have to leave you with that. Nothing else needs to be said – or effectively could be.

Introducing Median-omics - The Study of Life in the Middle

[Note: another controversial and over-long essay for the Addendum, one which works to explain my understanding of how life is operating for us currently. Again, please test these ideas for yourself before you try to apply them to life around you. If they make immediate sense and help you live better right away – cheers!]

Median-omics is an interesting study.

The study of life in the middle. It's lacked a name so far, even though it's principles are well known and practiced. No one has tried to put it all into one framework before – but it touches all of our lives.

It's been known mostly by it's results: the mundane, the average, the hum-drum, the mediocre. And as much as it's been run down, it's the way the vast majority of us live our lives.

But practically, it runs the planet, produces the majority of the goods, and consumes them in turn. The subject of Median-omics actually runs this humankind planet we live on.

The study of life in the middle. A simple definition (and graphical) is found in the Bell Curve. It's all that big hump in the middle which researchers found are in neither extreme.

Practically, it really looks like a 3D bump -like one you run over in your average car - as there are all sorts of extremes out on the edge with that great common bump in the middle. Most of our academia (itself an extreme) only compares two different types of things, instead of studying a universe of them all at once. But that's how we live our lives – the law of averages surplus in technicolor.

What does Median-omics cover?

Just about everything. Politics, Religion, Government, Celebrities, Economics, Media, you name it.

Because Median-omics studies involve the middle ground. It involves what is routinely popular and common sense. It comes from finding the "median" or the middle.

But it also includes the study of extremist edges, the fads, the oddball stuff that winds up in Freakonomics books.

It's easiest to explain if we cover some examples.

What Wal-Mart, Dubya and Obama Have in Common

Sam Walton found the "sweet spot" of merchandizing by finding out how to offer and deliver most of what everyone wants for just a little bit less than anyone else. He started it out in the Middle West, where big store chains like J.C. Penney, Sears and Montgomery Ward had settled long ago and become complacent, fat, and lazy. They were also shrinking.

Walton apprenticed in Penney's, got a business degree in University of Missouri, and set up his business operations in Arkansas. This was contrary to the "conventional wisdom" of all time. No one starts and expands a national (and now multinational) business out of Flyover Country (except the very Median-omic Warren Buffett). But the business model was the one which made the success.

You won't find specialty items in Wal-Mart – just the usual stuff you can find anywhere. Sure, they'll stock some extremely popular items, but once they quit selling, they are off the shelves and sent back to be remaindered. Merchandizing is a very cut-throat, black-and-white business.

Because average people have average needs. While they will buy flat-screen TV's, they also buy a whole lot more soap, tires, and dog food. So finding suppliers who can give decently priced goods and then have them set up their headquarters and warehouses next to yours in the middle of nowhere is actually a win-win all around. If you study Wal-Mart's hub-and-spoke distribution in conjunction with his sales strategies, you'll see exactly how brilliant this guy was.

The key point is that he's selling to the middle, with prices that they can afford – and keeping it all under one roof as a convenience. Same way with expanding into groceries.

The study of life in the middle.

Bush and Obama were elected with pluralities (well, mostly) – so they knew how to tell the middle of the country what they wanted to hear. Both of them had decidedly different coalitions of middle-ground supporters, but nonetheless, they were popular when elected. But both were found to be polarizing extremists, who dropped in popularity rapidly. Subsequently this made it hard to get anything done. Both spent a lot (LOT) of our taxpayer money in order to get a lot of support from Washington cronies, but this made them extremely unpopular outside the Beltway. (Because we voted them in to act like we do – and spending borrowed money we know isn't very wise.)

But they both applied Wal-Mart marketing (Median-omically speaking) of telling the bulk of the people what they wanted to hear. But this talk of bipartisanship really gets annoying after awhile. Because it's not possible. Both political parties are extremist – so they are unpopular, except within their hard-core middle.

What is popular (and always has been) is the independent middle. People who make up their own mind, regardless of what candidates say, and what party they are registered with. And they are usually "surprised" when some politician doesn't own up or follow up on their many promises. Because they are being told by politicians every two years (or weekly in a special interview on TV) exactly what political analysts think they wanted to hear.

But a funny accident happened when Bush cut taxes – revenue went up. Which means that to find the real sweet-spot of taxes, they have to keep cutting. People don't mind paying taxes as long as

1. they get something valuable back from it, and

2. it doesn't make things too expensive to buy or costs them their job.

No one knows what the popular level of taxation actually is. Because our politicians quit being average once they live in Washington for a few years. They turn into elite extremists. (Voter-enforced term limits usually cures that addiction.) Since most elected officials buy into the notion that spending other-people's money on your local pet-pork boondoggle is the way to get re-elected.

Not.

(And of course, both of these Presidents went to bad ends, since they both believed in *spending* themselves into oblivion...)

Where Obama screwed the pooch was in not staying Median-omic and pushing huge deficits and policies which alienated his own party and fueled the opposition. As a result, he laid the foundation for two divergent America's. The Median-omics of the greater land mass out-ruled the bi-coastal populations.

And, despite the predictions and support of the corporate "news" agencies for his successor, the usual Median-omic action of the 8-year switch of nominal power trumped their hopes to keep Obama's changes.

(Note: The media covered Obama's tail to keep him in office and appearing to be Median-omic. The fact that he ever produced only a fake birth certificate - that anyone trained in graphic arts could spot right off - and certain mounting evidence that he was a gay, closet Muslim and his wife was a transvestite with adopted children didn't help his case. Over the next few decades, there will be more scandalous details that surface, as the secrecy clamps he put on his school records dissolve. Obama was only Median-omic as a facade in order to get elected. He himself stated that he chose to be black. His father was mostly white according to their family tree. Amazing what the media will bury when it serves their own extreme interests.)

Median-omic Celebrities and the Long Tail

Chris Anderson has made a profitable study out of his "Long Tail" scenario. But he missed the most profitable point. The dull middle, where it's really the most profitable. At one end, the "tall head", you have celebrities and fads. Where a few people dominate one or two items and most of the advertising dollars to keep them there. For books, this means they have a steep curve up and just as steep down right after. They are blips on the radar. So any profit is made quickly – get in and get out. And too many are one-shot wonders – feast and then famine.

The Long Tail is the reverse. Very little profit made as you have to sell a lot of some very small-time sellers. Just as much total money changes hands, if not more – it's a whole lot of hands, though. If you were running a bookstore, you wouldn't keep a lot of these around. A brick-and-mortar store couldn't afford to keep hundreds of thousands of books available at any one time. The aggregate sales wouldn't keep the lights on. And so long tail books usually do best as print-on-demand.

What keeps stores restocking are the evergreen products which continue to sell, regardless. You'll find every bookstore in America (well, the bulk of them) sells some version or another of the Bible. Because people are always buying it. It's the hands-down all-time bestselling book in history. Because is appeals to the middle, the median consciousness of English-speaking peoples. No, it's not on the #1 spot every week. It just routinely sells. And sells. And sells.

So the real income to be made in book sales are authors like Napoleon Hill, whose books just continue to sell, regardless of whether they are marketed or not. These aren't Stephan King's, or J. K. Rowlings', or Dean Koonz' – they are really more the William Shakespeare's, Agatha Christie's, Barbara Cartland's, and Dr. Seuss's. No flash in the pan, but a consistent output of regular sellers – or one really good book based on common sense that just keeps selling regardless.

And if you look in any bookstore, you'll find that the latest fad sellers are out front and hyped up. But the bulk of their stock is in books who just continue to sell routinely at moderate amounts. Anything that doesn't sell is remaindered or discounted to get rid of it. Top-bottom-middle.

"Big Name" celebrities are mostly at the big head of this Long Tail. And you'll see them mostly burn-out and fade from the scene. Some of them are smart, like Fess Parker (Daniel Boone, Davy Crockett), and Alan Hale Jr. ("the Skipper" on Gilligan's Island) bought restaurants and lived comfortably. Others, like Jimmy Dean traded their fame for their own brand-name foods. The evergreen actors and actresses (as well as musicians) continue to have a nice living off of this. Dylan continues to churn out well-received hit albums, while infomercials are a nice income for those TV celebrities who were on for a very long time. What is normal for the stage and screen wouldn't be normal for you and I – but it can be a regular living like anything else. And the really long tail of celebrity-dom has people returning to their car sales or construction jobs after their one quasi-hit.

Median-omic Extremists, Gays, Acorn and Everyone Else

This study also embraces the extremists as necessary. Without them, life would be a bland bowl of lukewarm, un-salted oatmeal. Diversity is the spice of life.

But there is a caveat – don't expect because an extreme view is tolerated that it will ever be accepted. Homosexuals (Gay's, Lesbians, queers, fags, etc.) have never been and will never be mainstream. Nature has basically seen to that. And while there is every reason to give these their legal rights, they need to stay out of the mainstream in order to preserve those rights.

That seems odd, but it's true. Their main problem is that they aren't being allowed live a normal life in terms of hospital visitations, insurance, and so on. Otherwise, they've gotten everything they want, as long as they don't step on anyone else's toes – like dressing funny or scandalously, or playing loud music that keeps the neighborhood awake. Their real problem is that government and religion are too closely connected. Government took over the function of saying what a "marriage" is, which is actually Religion's function. If they would simply drop the marriage moniker and just be honest, saying that they are just actually licensors of civil unions, then this whole scene would go away. (Then, if you wanted to be married, go find a church that agrees with you, that you can be average in.)

The opposite effect happens when a President ignores broad swaths of the country in order to push an agenda that benefits only the extremes. While Obama directed and ordered various laws to be illegally ignored, subverted, or re-written by regulation, he was the most over-turned President in history. He lost more cases in the courts than any other. And his successor has even at this early point in 2017 already removed the bulk of these by either counter order, the cooperation of Congress to deal with his many "midnight" regulations, and many more orders and regulations simply do not have to be defended as they work their way through the courts.

The party in power only continues to rule as long as they also listen to middle as well as the extremes. That's Median-omic politics defined.

The laws of the land have to consult the continuing Median-omic values of the nation as a whole in order to be upheld.

You'll find an interesting thing happening with the old Civil Rights movement. They went mainstream, got nearly everything they wanted corrected, and now are busy turning conservative and building their own "good old boy" networks. When some flock-less "Reverend" tries to start a protest rally for some imagined "right" that was stepped on, you'll see only a handful turn out. The extreme became part of the middle and now has little to complain about overall.

Now, when some extremists get into power, they often find themselves isolated. Mostly where they don't quickly learn to become mainstream in their actions. Especially in this Internet Age. Acorn is a poster-child for this. Better get respectable if you are in the spot light – or you get defunded. If they'd studied what happened to the National Endowment for the Arts, they would have known. An example of doing this right was former-president Bill Clinton, who quickly learned to turn everything the Republican Congress approved into his idea. And we got the excesses of Welfare corrected, plus some other stuff. The worst presidential example so far was Millard Fillmore, who wouldn't listen to even his own party – a real extremist, elected because he looked and sounded "Presidential."

While Obama is currently busy trying to return to his community agitator/organizer role with a nation-wide network of trained protesters, the media who supported him is now being slowly exposed for the continual lies they have been telling. And those protesters have shown to be ineffective, regardless of their violence, intolerance, and bigotry.

The Median-omic view of this is "Live and Let Live." Anything that threatens a peaceful co-existence is quietly voted out of office. Rioters have long been found to be mostly from other cities than the one they were trashing. Analysis of the Democratic party's losses from decades of supporting extreme views shows little hope for them regaining a majority status that they had when Obama was rushed into office.

But we'll have to see what happens. As I update this, we are only a month into the 4-year term of his replacement and the dust is still flying. The best prediction I've heard is that the Democrats will propose an extremist in 2020, and then a more Median-omic candidate for 2024. Again, we'll have to wait and see.

The Zen of a Median-omic Lifestyle

If you started applying this to your own life, you'd quickly find that this is actually the most economical way to live. And the happiest and most sensible.

The government is actually telling you to be average. If you look over the tax code carefully, you'll see they are also telling you to start a business and work for yourself – that's where the real low taxes are. And you'll see that the bulk of the jobs in the U.S. are created and maintained by small businesses. That's what makes every recovery in a recession. When you make it harder for the bulk of your small businesses to get started, you are damping everything down.

But a living by Median-omics actually puts you into a sort of "Zone." While you don't have to be a big fan of Alan Watts, he did cover very simple explanations of Zen – which are applicable in any Median-omics lifestyle. Your best interests are served by just enjoying the life you currently live. While you understand and empathize with the extremes, you actually live in the middle. And you live to experience your own life, not based on what "celebrities", or politicians, or Wall Street CEO's do with their lives – or any other extreme minority group. Your decisions are your own. People who stick with their traditional lifestyles live very mundane, but happy lives.

Like the credit card binge we all are now suffering through as well as the sub-prime mortgage mess our politicians got us into. We erred by moving from traditionally successful finances of savings and lay-a-ways. So the credit card industry now looks to be a blip on the radar. Politicians meanwhile tried to get more votes by pressuring finance companies to make risky loans to people who had never done anything before besides pay rent. Because home ownership was equated with a "right". But it's always been a privilege you earn. Always will be. And these guys crashed the economy (don't worry, some group or another does this every 6-8 years like clockwork.)

If you stick to what works, what's common sense, then you live a simple and happy life. You aren't striving to keep up with all these fads going. You don't dress like celebrities or cult guru's. And you read the stories of stars and starlets who ruin their lives or kill themselves off over drugs or fast cars or psychotic lovers. Most of us don't. And that's living in the Zen of the Median-omic middle.

Just be normal and enjoy it.

Median-omic Predictions

So, now you can predict what is going to happen:

- Every time one political party gets in power, they lose it rapidly. Always have a president of one party and a Congress of the other. Do nothing while they're there.

- Extremists who threaten the middle (Islamic and other terrorists) will get wiped out. Not popular, as they don't allow the average lifestyle to continue.

- If you are in a Long Tail group (Gays, Vegans, Environmental and animal "rights" activists) – make it easy to be compromised with in order to get what you want. Don't run a campaign that everyone should live like you do. Just say you want to be left alone to live your own life. Those that do, can. But don't try to get the government to support your cause. Like organic farming, it usually gives you a result you don't want – and no one else does, either.

- People who want to get elected (a form of celebrity) will stay in office only as long as they are "normal" to their constituents – and really accomplish nothing. You get a lifetime pension and benefits automatically, so why work at standing out from the crowd and risk being defeated in a primary?

And some advice about what you should be doing with your life:

- Use your common sense to pick your own careful path –
  and you can be in the "zone" all the time.

- Forget about listening to the mass media guru's or news
  announcers who are constantly telling you the sky is
  falling. Realize that the sun will come up tomorrow, and
  the day after, and even the day after that. Those
  extremists live by selling advertising to pitch products
  to the average Joe and Joleen – so they want to hook
  you into watching their shows in between commercials.
  Talk and listen to your neighbor on your block – you
  know them, the ones who have a house almost like
  yours...

- Vote for people who think and act like you do – and
  then hold their feet to the fire. If we had average Joes
  and Joanna's rotating through our elected positions
  (and maybe all government positions), we'd start having
  more common sense actions showing up – and maybe
  some real service, as well.

- Start ignoring all conventional wisdom and see if going
  the exact opposite way isn't more profitable.

Because the trick to being happy in this seemingly chaotic
world we live in is to luxuriate in the average, common-place
stuff that surrounds you. Realize that the average people
actually rule this planet, not the titular leaders who change
every few years. People vote with their pocket books and
wallets and remote controls. Understand that any real power in
this country probably starts right there in your own
neighborhood.

The next time some community-organizing activist comes
around who says that you should go out and stand up for what
is "right" and "make a difference" – that your purpose for living
is to get your face on the evening news for the cause they are
pushing... just quietly smile and nod and show them the door.
But when that sales man comes in and says that if you buy "X"
detergent because everyone else does – usher him in and get

him some coffee and cakes. He's telling you how great you are for just being yourself.

Index

Table of Contents

Bonus

Get No-Charge Access to Bestselling Success Guides from Our Online Library

(for a limited time only)

Instant Access - Join Here

Click or type into your browser:

http://livesensical.com/go/freelibrary/

Made in the USA
Middletown, DE
14 January 2020